AF572227

Mainstream Access, Inc.
Industry Guides Project Staff

Project Director-Administration:
Richard J. Pilder, Ph.D.

Project Director-Editorial:
William F. Pilder, Ph.D.

Mainstream Access, Inc., created and directed by Richard J. Pilder, Ph.D., and William F. Pilder, Ph.D., is a New York–based career consulting firm with offices in Philadelphia and Stamford, Connecticut. It specializes in career opportunity development and marketing for individuals. The company is also well known in the field of corporate outplacement services. The series of industry Guides of which this book is part are products of Mainstream Access, Inc.

Richard J. Pilder, Ph.D.,
and William F. Pilder, Ph.D.,
Directors of Mainstream Access, Inc.

HOW TO FIND YOUR LIFE'S WORK

STAYING OUT OF TRAPS AND TAKING CONTROL OF YOUR CAREER

PRENTICE-HALL, INC., Englewood Cliffs, New Jersey 07632

Library of Congress Cataloging in Publication Data

Pilder, Richard J.
How to find your life's work.

(Job finder series) (A Spectrum Book)
Includes bibliographical references and index.
1. Vocational guidance. 2. Job hunting. I. Pilder, William. II. Title. III. Series.
HF5381.P54 650.1'4 81-7297
ISBN 0-13-406710-X AACR2
ISBN 0-13-406702-9 (pbk.)

This Spectrum Book can be made available to businesses and organizations at a special discount when ordered in large quantities. For more information, contact: Prentice-Hall, Inc., General Book Marketing, Special Sales Division, Englewood Cliffs, New Jersey 07632.

Editorial/production supervision by Carol Smith
Interior design by Christine Gehring Wolf
Cover design by Honi Werner
Manufacturing buyer: Barbara A. Frick

A SPECTRUM BOOK

10 9 8 7 6 5 4 3 2 1

Printed in the United States of America

Prentice-Hall International, Inc., *London*
Prentice-Hall of Australia Pty. Limited, *Sydney*
Prentice-Hall of Canada, Ltd., *Toronto*
Prentice-Hall of India Private Limited, *New Delhi*
Prentice-Hall of Japan, Inc., *Tokyo*
Prentice-Hall of Southeast Asia Pte. Ltd., *Singapore*
Whitehall Books Limited, *Wellington, New Zealand*

". . . the fundamental criterion for comparing social, economic and political systems is not and cannot be the criterion of hegemony and imperialism.

It can be—and indeed it must be—the humanistic criterion, namely the measure in which each system is really capable of reducing, restraining and eliminating, as far as possible, the various forms of exploitation of man, and of insuring for him through work not only the just distribution of the indispensable material goods, but also a participation, in keeping with his dignity, in the whole process of production and in the social life that grows up around that process.

Disturbing factors are frequently present in the form of the frightful disparities between excessively rich individuals and groups on the one hand and, on the other hand, the majority made up of the poor or, indeed, of the destitute, who lack food and opportunities for work and education, and are in great numbers condemned to hunger and disease.

And concern is also caused at time by the radical separation of work from property, by immense indifference to the production enterprise to which he is linked only by work obligation without feeling that he's working for a good that will be his or for himself.

It is no secret that the abyss separating the minority of the excessively rich from the multitude of the destitute is a very grave symptom in the life of any society. This also must be said—with even greater insistence—with regard to the abyss separating countries and regions of the earth."

Pope John Paul II
Address before the United Nations
2 October 1979

The nonaligned countries stress the fact that it is imperative to do away with the enormous inequality that separates the developed from the developing countries. We are struggling for an eradication of poverty, of hunger, disease and illiteracy from which hundreds of millions of human beings still suffer. We aspire to a new world order—one based on justice, on equity and peace, one that will replace the unjust and unequal system which prevails today in which, as proclaimed in the final declaration at Havana, "wealth is still concentrated in the hands of a few powers whose wasteful economies are maintained by the exploitation of the labor as well as the transfer and the plunder of the national and other resources of the peoples of Africa, Latin America, Asia and other regions of the world."

According to statistical information, the world is making an annual investment in military expenditures of more than $300 billion. With $300 billion you could in one year build 600,000 schools with a capacity for 400 million children, or you could build 60 million comfortable homes for 300 million people, or you could build 30,000 hospitals with 18 million beds, or you could build 20,000 factories with jobs for more than 20 million workers, or you could build irrigation systems to water 150 million hectares of land, which with the appropriate technology, could feed a billion people.

Mankind wastes this much every year on its military spending. Moreover, consider further the enormous amount of human resources in full use of technicians, of scientists, as a squandering and wasting of fuel, raw materials and other items.

This is the fabulous price of preventing a true climate of confidence and peace from existing in the world. The United States alone will in the 1980's spend six times this much on military activities.

We are requesting less for 10 years of development than is spent in a single year by the ministries of war and much less than a tenth of what will be spent for military purposes in 10 years.

Fidel Castro
Address before the United Nations
12 October 1979

CONTENTS

3

HOW ORGANIZATIONS FUNCTION AND WHERE YOU FIT, 38

4

ORGANIZATIONAL NEEDS AND CAREER DEVELOPMENT, 61

5

REFRAMING THE JOB SEARCH: NETWORKING, 83

INTRODUCTION

This book begins a series. Its intent is to help you determine the direction you should take in choosing, establishing, and developing your career. Considerable work has been done in the last ten years to develop techniques that enable you to assess your capabilities, interests, and specific skills in order to develop effective strategies for doing a job search. This book and the series it begins are designed to complement this work in two ways. First, the self-assessment techniques of the past stop short of linking you to specific organizational functions. They also fail to connect you with the bigger issues that go beyond mere self-concern and affect the planet as a whole. The series starts by giving you a method for considering career planning within this larger context. It also provides a way of linking your interests to organizational functions as a first step to situating yourself within a particular industry.

Once you have an idea of the industry you are interested in, you need up-to-date industry-based information. That is where the rest of the books in the series come in: they are Guides to specific fields and industries. A great deal of information exists on different occupations, but it is widely scattered or buried in highly specialized sources that are practically inaccessible and so unwieldy as to be almost useless to the general reader. Experience is necessary just to make sense out of the information that is around. The individual industry guides in our series are designed to solve this problem. They synthesize such information as: what the industry does, the various functions or specializations within the industry evaluated by task and salary, names of leading firms, consultants who specialize in that industry, leading professional associations, directories, examples of successful people, typical entry-level positions as well as opportunities for mid-career changers, latest developments, and trends that create career opportunities. All of this information will be updated as the need arises.

This makes the series, taken together, a package of value for graduating college students making the transition from school to work, or for college students early in their studies who wish to plan their courses around a specific career. Women seeking to enter the job market after some years of child rearing will find the series a good source of direction for their search. If you are considering a career change, you will find a special section in each Guide addressed to your needs. If you are retiring and seek a meaningful second career, the series will assist your transition. Finally, professionals within the industries surveyed by the Guides might appreciate the overview and synthesis of information provided.

Chapter 1 of this book talks about career development as it relates to personal change. It is based on the thesis that you can't have one without the other. Effective career development necessitates personal change of a fundamental kind. This change entails the art of reframing, which is explained in the first chapter. *Chapter 2* presents a method for career planning in the context of a bigger picture involving personal, organizational and global needs considered simultaneously. The perspective of this entire series is that the coming decade demands such holistic planning. The method enables you to see how you function in relation to the whole—the whole of you as well as the whole of the planet. This method is specifically related to the issues of adult development at mid-life when career shifts often occur or should occur. *Chapter 3* then presents a model of how organizations work, giving an overview of the functions in which career paths are situated. It will help you link your direction to a specific organizational function and assist your job search. *Chapter 4* explores the relation of individual styles of functioning to the basic changes occurring in organizations that make up our present culture. These are the changes that offer you the most significant career opportunities. *Chapter 5,* on networking, shows you how to use the information given in the Guides for doing successful job search.

At the heart of the entire series is the fundamental belief that work ought to have personal meaning; that it should be more than merely something we do for eight hours a day to get money to exchange for needed goods and services. This rests on the added conviction that such meaning comes from being involved in something whose scope goes beyond the limits of one's own day-to-day satisfaction. In virtually every industry today there are developments and needs emerging that relate to the most important issues now facing the planet. You can build and design your career opportunities around these needs, thereby participating in the kind of planetary citizenship that has become an imperative of the present moment in history. The eighties are already being described as the "Dangerous Decade," given the nature of the world economy, the energy crisis, and the ever-present threat of superpower confrontation. Having a sense that your work is related to the larger issues can restore the concept of *vocation* to career planning. The word itself is not often used these days; it is derived from the Latin root *vocare,* which means to call. To be able to hear the call of these planetary issues and relate your own work to them can provide a sense of vocation. Without this sense, work and its various career expressions lack depth and genuine meaning.

Each Guide in this series has been carefully researched to assemble within its pages the most recent information available on each industry and relate it to the major issues now affecting careers in the field. As a whole, the series is a first step in the development of an information service designed to provide industry-based data on career opportunities and human resources planning. It is hoped that this volume and the accompanying series of industry Guides will help you and others to plan your own career in this larger perspective.

CAREER DEVELOPMENT AND PERSONAL CHANGE: REFRAMING

PURPOSE

When man was a hunter, he had personal control over his work. With survival as the motivating force, he provided for his family and himself as best he could and derived all the satisfactions—and agonies—of being involved in a process whose rewards were immediate and evident. Even through the Middle Ages, whether as a farmer or as a craftsman in the Guilds, he kept his involvement in the totality of his work and experienced the dignity that accompanies being master of what you do. Of course, the feudal system had its evils, by which groups and their labor were exploited, but it was only with the Industrial Revolution that man was violently deprived of control over his work. This revolution created the technological progress that has permitted entire societies to move beyond subsistence economies. That is, for the most part, people in the developed countries no longer worry about survival, yet something fundamental about life has been lost. Man no longer controls his work; he does not benefit directly from what he produces. Karl Marx, of course, saw this clearly, and the upheaval his thinking has created can be related to the seriousness of man's being torn from control over his work. The dignity that goes with being master of our work is so fundamental that its loss can only create outrage. Unfortunately, the system is such that frequently the outrage can neither find an effective outlet nor be channeled into action that rectifies the situation, so it turns inward to create depression and despair. Studs Terkel's *Working* is a document describing how rampant this despair has become in the highly developed society of the United States.*

In our thumbnail sketch of the history of work, you can see the paradoxes facing anyone concerned with a meaningful career. Progress since the Industrial Revolution has enabled us to be free enough from the demands of survival to be able to think about our work. Yet that very progress has wrenched from us control of our work, and it is this control that gives it dignity. We can't reverse the trends that have created these problems; we can transform our lives by engaging in the effort to assume control over what we do. In the struggle to accomplish this, we can be free of the despair that clouds so much of our working lives today.

Over the last ten years some progress has been made in enabling us to take more control of our working lives at every stage. The purpose of this chapter is to discuss what is needed to achieve this control, especially the personal changes required for successful career development. The basic thesis of this chapter is that career development, specifically, acquiring more control over your work, requires fundamental personal change. A raft of data has appeared in the last decade revealing society's widespread dissatisfaction with work: its monotony, its stifling of creativity, its general deadening effects. However, most career handbooks merely offer techniques (sometimes merely gimmicks) for getting a better job. The fundamental issues of how to bring about changes on both personal and organizational levels are often overlooked. Without these basic changes, there can be no genuine career development and work continues to lack meaning.†

CHANGE AS REFRAMING, OR GETTING OUT OF BOXES

It is never easy to learn to see things differently and then to act in new ways related to the new perceptions. Basically, two changes are

* Studs Terkel, *Working* (New York: Avon, 1975).

† Richard Nelson Bolles, *What Color is Your Parachute?* (Berkeley, California: Ten Speed Press, revised, 1977). The work of John Crystal and Richard Bolles addresses the need for personal change in relation to career transitions. It stands out clearly among the raft of more gimmicky, superficial writing about careers. We will refer to it at various points in this chapter.

required in the effort to take control of your working life. First, the way in which you view yourself—the box you have put yourself in or have been put in—must change. Second, you must get out of the box of the employment system.*

Getting out of boxes is no easy matter. Only the creative minority are capable of acting outside the boxes in which the majority are trapped. In order to understand just what is involved in getting free of the various boxes that hem in creativity and individuality, it is worthwhile to consider the change process.

Some valuable work on change as a process has come out of the Brief Therapy Center connected with the Mental Research Institute in Palo Alto, California.† The Center was established in 1966 to investigate the phenomena of human change. At the heart of this work is the idea of *reframing,* which is referred to as "the gentle art." This notion is most relevant to career development and a convenient method for summarizing the personal changes required. Reframing is what enables anyone to jump free of boxes—in this context, the box of the employment system and the "single career imperative."‡

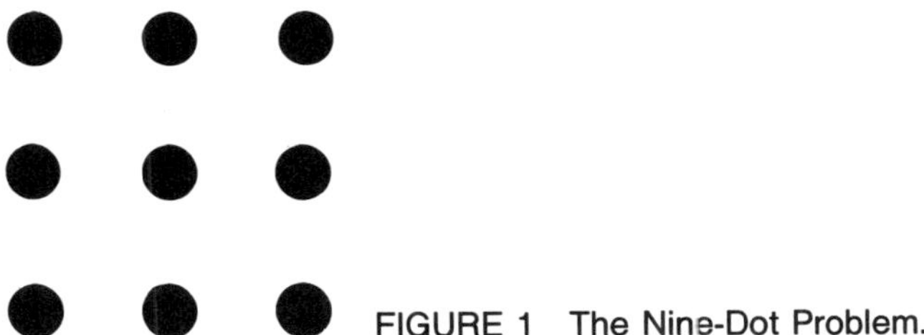

FIGURE 1 The Nine-Dot Problem.

To begin to understand what reframing means, consider Figure 1, the Nine-Dot Problem. Study the arrangement of dots in the problem, then see if you can connect the nine dots using only four straight lines. Once you begin, do not lift your pencil from the paper. Before reading further, try to solve the problem. The solution will mean much more if you have struggled to discover it.

Many people bring a self-imposed box to this problem that prevents its solution. No matter what is tried in the way of connected lines inside the box, no solution is found. Only by allowing yourself to go outside the box of the nine-dot configuration is the solution possible. The solu-

* Richard Nelson Bolles, *The Three Boxes of Life and How to Get Out of Them* (Berkeley, California: Ten Speed Press, 1978).

† Paul Watzlawick, John Weakland, and Richard Fisch, *Change* (New York: W. W. Norton & Company, 1974).

‡ Seymor B. Sarason, *Work, Aging and Social Change: Professionals and the One Life–One Career Imperative* (New York: Free Press, 1977).

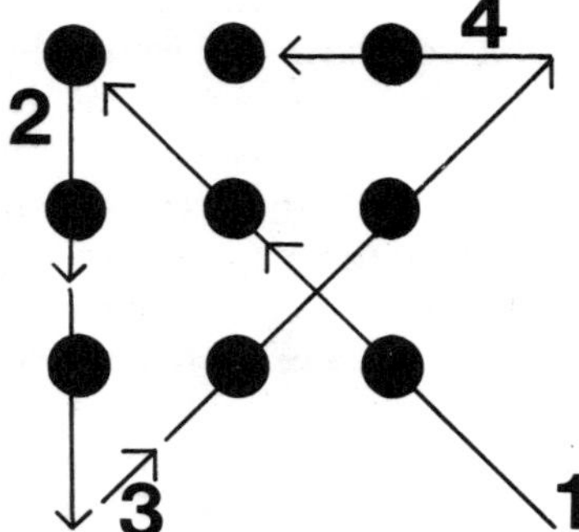

FIGURE 2 Solution of the Nine-Dot Problem.

tion requires a reframing of the standard approach to drawing the connecting lines. Specifically, the length of the lines must extend beyond the box.

REFRAMING AND CAREER

If the notion of reframing is applied to the problem of developing your career or even the issue of job hunting, it is possible to examine the old frames that are debilitating as well as the new frameworks that make possible the changes which lead to controlling your career. Throughout this section, you may find Figure 3 a helpful aid. Most people impose a box on themselves in relation to their career. The box has the basic characteristics shown in the illustration.

The Old Frames

1. *You are limited to past experience.* Experience here is usually defined as having been formally employed in a particular area. Want ads, classifieds, employment agency announcements, executive search talk, etc., strongly reinforce this framework. A person new to the job market or unemployed for a while is especially limited. The same is true for students looking for their first career opportunity after leaving school.

2. *You must follow established procedures* to secure employment. Read ads, send résumés, fill out applications, use "contacts," or go to agencies—these procedures create a passivity and lack of control over the whole process that proves to be demoralizing.

3. *Passivity.* Wait for responses, submit to procedures, be interviewed.

	YOU	EMPLOYMENT SYSTEM
OLD FRAME	Limited to past experience Limited to following established procedures of employment system Lacking "contacts" Passive	Publicly announces available positions Received applicants through personnel department procedures, otherwise impenetrable and inaccessible Single career imperative.
NEW FRAME	In possession of skills that transfer to a number of fields Capable of deciding independently what to do, where, and able to make it happen Skilled at networking and the research that goes with it Active/in control	80% of opportunities are hidden Positions are often created A network of persons who are accessible directly, especially the decision-making in regard to hiring.

FIGURE 3 Reframing As Applied to You and the Employment System.

Parallel to this box for the self is the *employment system box,* which has these characteristics.

1. *Single career imperative.* There is something suspicious about anyone who changes careers. "By all means, keep on that track," is the command built into the employment system judgments.

2. *Available positions are publicly announced* in newspapers, journals, etc. They are also registered with employment agencies of various kinds or placed with executive search firms.

3. *Applications made directly to companies.* These are made through the personnel department and its established hiring procedures.

4. *The employment system is impenetrable.* Beyond the open door of personnel departments, employment systems are impenetrable and largely inaccessible.

Your New Frames

It is these old boxes or frameworks that you must become conscious of in order to enable you to create new frames. For you the new frame provides the following characteristics which relate to how you see yourself in relation to career and employment.

1. Your skills can be identified along with specific accomplishments that are transferable to a variety of work settings.

2. You have the power to decide what you want to do, where you want to do it, and the ability to act toward the decision makers in any particular organization.

3. You can be skilled in researching the field of your interest and capable of networking professionals in that field in preparation for employment.

4. In short, the new frame enables you to be *active* and *in control* of your working life.

One of the basic tools for accomplishing this particular reframing is the work/life autobiographical statement used extensively by John Crystal and referred to by Bolles. In *Where Do I Go from Here with My Life?** the two collaborate in presenting a systematic method of developing the autobiographical statement and using it for skill identification as well as accomplishment listings. They suggest preparing an extensive autobiographical statement, two hundred or more pages, where you tell in great detail all you have accomplished so far. This lengthy statement should then be broken down and analyzed so as to identify the specific skills which you have used successfully over time. There is significant power in such storytelling, and the possibility of reframing your view of yourself is greatly enhanced. Ira Progoff's Journal method is another powerful tool that in some ways complements Crystal in its appreciation for deeper forces that influence life.† The writings of Crystal and Bolles, as well as many others, contain various exercises and techniques directed at self-assessment. They are all designed to assist you in creating a new view of yourself as you plan your career.

First-Order Change versus Second-Order Change

It should be noted here that the mere doing of these exercises, the use of these tools, does not guarantee a way out of the old framework.

* John C. Crystal and Richard N. Bolles, *Where Do I Go from Here with My Life?* (New York: Seabury Press, 1974).

† Ira Progoff, *At a Journal Workshop* (New York: Dialogue House Library, 45 West 10th Street, 1975).

In the work on change as a process mentioned earlier, the authors distinguish between *first-order* and *second-order* change. They call first-order change doing "more of the same." It's when you try a lot of things, but stay in the original box. Second-order change occurs when there is actual reframing. The old box is truly gone and you begin acting in new ways. What enables you to move from first-order change to second-order is still very much a mystery. Science does not have the exact explanation. Reframing is an art that comes out of a process which is greatly enhanced by careful telling of your story. The method for doing this telling can vary, depending on how much you are aware of yourself, but the autobiographical statement has proven to be a definite help for many toward the necessary reframing. Such exercises aid the move from first- to second-order change. They do not, however, connect you with meaning in your work. That only comes when you see how your personal endeavors relate to a larger context. The tools that will be presented here are specifically designed to complement self-assessment techniques by providing methods for considering how your work relates to the whole. Then meaning is possible which further supports second-order change, a kind of change that is never easy. Without the support of meaning it is impossible to experience second-order change. Meaning leads you through all the forces resistant to change, both within yourself and within the organizations that make up the employment system. These forces that work against your getting out of the old boxes are indeed formidable. As you saw in the beginning of this chapter, industrialization and specialization have torn most people from work that has dignity.

True craftsmanship and quality work in any human endeavor depends upon your being in control of what you produce, not being merely a means to production. Productivity and quality of working life—those much talked about issues—depend upon the empowering of the individual in regard to career. In the seventies, a growing number of people began considering their careers and how to get out of their own boxes. The eighties will require the large organizations that make up the global workplace to provide opportunity for their workers to have more say over their careers. Fewer and fewer people are content with the old boxes. Recent surveys on the changing attitudes of workers confirm this discontent, and observers are now talking about the emerging new breed of worker.*

It appears that this reevaluation is global in scope and is affecting the workplace in every nation. Management must be aware of this move-

* Michael R. Cooper, Brian S. Morgan, Patricia M. Foley, and Leon B. Kaplan, "Changing Employee Values: Deepening Discontent?" *Harvard Business Review* (January–February 1979), 117–125.

ment to reframing, and it must respond creatively by adopting some reframing of its own. There are significant energies being released by these changes in individuals that could be used for renewing organizations, if management is capable of creative and understanding responses. The alternative is growing alienation in the workplace and a further decline in productivity. It is this dimension of the productivity problem that deserves more and more urgent attention from management levels who have been asleep to it so far. The popularity of career development activity of all kinds is a signal to organizations about the reframing *they* are in need of in order to relate to the new breed of worker.

Reframing for the Professional Woman

Another related signal to organizations is the growing number of women entering professional ranks. In order to act in the ways necessary to successfully enter and compete in today's job market, a woman usually must experience second-order change. A lot of cultural boxes must be discarded containing old definitions of how a woman is supposed to be, especially in relation to men. The fact that significant numbers of women have already discarded these old frameworks is a phenomenon of profound importance for organizations and the men who, by and large, still run them. The person who has experienced second-order change knows a great deal more about the whole of reality than someone who has remained in the frameworks into which she was thrown at birth. The woman who has chosen a career has often gone through significant transformation. She has gotten into an organization and frequently does know more about the whole than those who are leading her. In this context, a major aspect of the development of organizations in the next decade will potentially be led by the professional woman who by way of cultural experience and what she has been through sees more. This is not to say that there aren't men who know the reality of second-order change—there are, of course, many. However, most such men become involved in more creative or marginal endeavors. The men who concentrate on the fast tracks to the top of the career ladders which make up the major organizations are frequently not familiar with second-order change. This situation is producing a creative tension or polarity in organizational life that promises to be one of the significant dimensions of change for the near future.

In some ways, the creative tension just described should provide encouragement to women seeking entry to today's job market. The reframing they must experience is more complex and difficult, yet their contribution will be more important over the next decade, especially if they are true to their experience. A number of recent works on women in management seem to suggest that to be successful women should imitate men, play their games. The point of view here, and one which will be more fully developed in the next chapter, is that the neglected functions in organizational life are those which are most fully developed in the majority of women in this culture. The direction of development is by way of the neglected side of a personality, which points to a major aspect of woman's contribution to organizational life in the future. More about this in Chapter 2. The important point here is that second-order change is worth struggling toward because it creates an awareness of the whole which makes for leadership. The individual who has gone through such change constitutes a part of an important creative segment out of which leadership comes. Certainly there have already been significant changes wrought by women in the major organizations in which work takes place. Equal rights consciousness at management levels is radically different today due to the powerful presence of the career woman.

The Importance of Creativity

A major aspect of acting out of your new frame has to do with creativity. Central to the creative act is the ability to see things in a brand new way. What you see in any situation is partly a function of what you bring to it—your frameworks. The first step toward creative action is to become aware of the frameworks that you habitually use and start to discover new ones. Did you ever notice how differently the world looks through the frame a camera imposes? Consider carefully the new frame for the self in Figure 3. It requires you to take complete control of your working life and eliminate the frustrating and ineffective passivity characteristic of standard approaches to the employment system. However, seeing this new frame and acting out of it are two different things. As in all personal change, insight is not enough. It may provide the beginning of change, but there is no substitute for action. Fear and uncertainty create barriers that you must break through in order to act out of a new framework. The action prescribed in the pages that follow, especially Chapter 5 on networking, provides details on how you can reframe your approach.

The other aspect of the new frame for the self has to do with research and information-gathering related to your intended career field. This is crucial to the new frame; there is considerable work that needs to be done to develop the kind of information needed for career and job search purposes. The major intent of this book and the guides that complement it is to start providing this kind of support, as well as showing a method for researching specific industries that you can learn to use on your own. The effort here is to complement the work of the last decade by picking up the research and information needs as they relate to effective linking of individuals to the organizational expression of work. Networking is successful when the job seeker has quality information to give. This is a major part of acting in new and effective ways and constitutes what needs to be the focus of a great deal of future work.

A NEW FRAME FOR THE EMPLOYMENT SYSTEM

Related to your personal new frame is a new way of viewing the employment system. Its characteristics change considerably when viewed from this perspective.

1. The employment system is a network of persons directly accessible when intelligently approached. This network has both relevant information on recent developments as well as the power to hire competent personnel.

2. Positions are frequently created when needs arise or good people appear, as the network in a particular field nourishes and develops itself.

3. Due to the essential nature of the employment network—how its linkages connect and how information flows—most opportunities are never formally made visible. This is simply another way of viewing the "hidden job market." In this way of viewing employment systems, you are empowered to control them and choose how you wish to relate to them. As a network, they take on life and a personal dimension, rather than the demeaning, impersonal characteristics so often encountered in the old way of searching for a job. The full implications of this new way of viewing the employment system will be examined in detail in Chapter 5 on networking.

SUMMARY

Reframing of oneself and the employment system is the essence of the change that must be experienced in order to give individuals more control over their careers. The reframing that is called for requires real personal change, what was referred to in this chapter as "second-order change." Such change only comes about when you truly jump free of the box in which you happen to be trapped. It begins with the creative act of becoming aware of your personal framework. Only by getting completely out of the old box does genuine change happen. Then you take charge of your own working life. This kind of change is the necessary beginning for anyone who wants to design a personal career plan or direction. Though necessary as a start, it is alone insufficient. It is also necessary to develop a clear knowledge of the industry and organizations that make up that field in which a career is being planned. The individual who doesn't know the territory cannot cover it effectively.

Most of the important work on careers done during the last decade focuses on the individual and the changes needed at the personal level. When it comes to knowledge about industries and their various organizations, there is a vast sea of information, making it quite difficult to link personal career objectives to practical organizational needs in a specific industry. Knowing exactly what you want to do depends on having a practical place in which to do it for the self-knowledge to be worth while. Also, what you want should have some relationship to what is needed socially as well as organizationally. In order to complement the work of the past ten years regarding the individual's career concerns, this series intends to provide an information service that is industry-based. In the chapters of this book which follow are some tools to guide you in using this information in the particular industry in which you have career interests. Effective use of the information requires that you link personal skills, abilities, and interests to a function or industry. You should then be able to do an effective job search employing that information.

CAREER PLANNING: SEEING THE BIGGER PICTURE

PURPOSE

There is a well known tale about two men walking down the same road carrying stones. One of them, in being stopped and asked what he was doing, replied: "I'm carrying stones." There was a hint of impatience and more than a little anger in the response. The other man when asked the same question answered calmly and with a smile: "I'm building a cathedral."

The meaning of your work depends upon how you see it in relation to the whole. Heraclitus said, "The way up is the way down"; this epigraph can be applied to career planning within the bigger picture. In the last chapter the emphasis was on what personal changes you need to accomplish in order to take control of your working life. This emphasis characterizes the concern with career which comes out of the seventies, and is in some ways typical of the focus of that decade. At best, the focus is centered on yourself in order to balance the impersonal nature of large bureaucratic systems so characteristic of Western culture. At its worst, it is merely narcissistic. Clearly, it is necessary for you to complement this perspective by emphasizing the relation of your concerns to the larger whole. As you saw in the last chapter, without this sense of the whole, work can be too easily ridden with despair and meaninglessness. In the present chapter this will be accomplished in two ways.

First, a method will be presented which enables you to look at the whole of yourself in relation to career. The method considers how you personally function with special attention being given to what you have so far neglected or excluded from your personality. Your future development depends upon being willing to consider what you have systematically left out in earlier years.

It is important to understand what is meant here by the words "excluded," "neglected," and "systematically left out." The nature of your development is such that the exclusion or neglect of approximately half of your powers is unavoidable, even necessary, as the consolidation of the personality takes place during the first years of life. There is no conscious, willed exclusion on your part, this is just the way development takes place. Your family plays an important role in encouraging you to be one way and not another. The school and your religion do likewise. School, religion, and family are expressions of a culture that also has its point of view. Western culture has neglected many aspects of the world in its effort to pursue its particular brand of science. The same is true of the culture of the East which has neglected the concerns of the Western world in the interest of pursuing its own path of development. Right now the West is beginning to recognize its need for the East and vice versa. For development to be complete, both need each other. The same is true on the personal plane. Your growth depends on recognizing your need for what has so far been excluded from your development.

Seeing this need and being willing to do something about it marks the beginning of adult development. It starts a type of learning that goes beyond what takes place in schools or organized religion, since it rests on direct experience of what you've been taught to exclude. It is this type of learning on your part that will enable bridges to be built between West and East—bridges that are vital to the next stage of development required of humanity. It is this basic understanding of your part in the nuturing of the whole of the planet that can provide meaning to your work.

The second way to complement the strict concern with self in making career decisions is to consider the major global issues facing each of us. There are developments taking place across the globe that relate to opposite forces meeting within the planetary whole. The Western world, as mentioned before, is beginning to return to what it has systematically neglected or excluded from its own growth. In its scientific effort to develop and control the material universe, it often left out spirit. The East likewise is reaching out for what it has neglected so far in its history. Though it tends to be less materialistic than the West, it needs technological development to overcome its poverty and squalor. These trends are profound and are significantly influencing life across the globe. An appreciation and renewed sense of responsibility for the planetary whole becomes possible only when we have faced the whole of ourselves. Being able to see how your personal career direction relates to the picture of the planetary whole and its needs makes it possible for you to be building cathedrals instead of carrying stones. It is also a practical way of planning your career on the basis of the major trends and needs occurring in the development of organizations worldwide. Throughout this chapter, the parallels which exist between your personal development and the development of the planetary whole will be drawn. Having this larger view is necessary if you are to discover a sense of vocation in your work. Each of us is entitled to just such a personal sense of vocation.

Skill Identification and Personal Awareness

In the work done so far in the career development field there is a great deal of emphasis on skill identification. Though this is a necessary part of gaining control over your work, it is insufficient for determining what you want to do. A clear sense of direction comes out of a deeper kind of self-examination carried out in the context of what is needed by the whole. Skills have to do with behavior, and a knowledge of how you behave may not produce a sense of direction. Therefore, to complement the efforts at skill identification, this chapter will employ a depth perspective on career development. By describing in detail how you function using this deeper perspective, you will have a second set of tools for determining your direction.

Values, beliefs, and other forces are beyond your control, yet most influential when it comes to how you behave. They are essential in determining your direction. At the depth level, opposites come into play—these are the major forces influencing your choices. At this time in history, when you see very few things outside yourself that are stable, this consideration of the opposites within you becomes even more necessary. Your concern with your career and its meaning is partly a function of the cultural upheaval occurring now that affects you at the deepest level. In viewing how you function in relation to the whole of your personality, you will have a way of relating to these deeper forces within you that complements the emphasis on skills or behavior. The method will also enable you to begin to consider what you have so far neglected in your development. In this way, your career development can be directly related to the demands of your personal development, as well as to the needs of the planet as a whole. Again, viewing this bigger picture will enable you to build cathedrals instead of merely carrying stones.

A METHOD FOR MAPPING HOW YOU FUNCTION

If, for just a few seconds, you could stop viewing the world the way you habitually view it, you might begin to realize how limited your horizons are. If you recall the Nine Dot problem, the solution may have evaded you only because you imposed the limitations of the box onto the problem. The box was *your* imposition. This sense of the limits of your personal world is the beginning of real adult learning. Let's consider how to develop a greater awareness of these limits.

As a way to begin, look at the brief list of words in Figure 4. Make the choices requested as spontaneously as you can before going on. This exercise will help you understand the theory that follows.

FIGURE 4 An Exercise in Word Choice.

Which word in each pair appeals to you more?

Circle either A or B.

1.	(A) firm	(B) warm
2.	(A) theory	(B) practice
3.	(A) construct	(B) invent
4.	(A) benefits	(B) blessings
5.	(A) convincing	(B) moving
6.	(A) statement	(B) concept
7.	(A) determined	(B) committed
8.	(A) facts	(B) ideas
9.	(A) practical	(B) imaginative
10.	(A) justice	(B) mercy
11.	(A) thoughts	(B) emotions
12.	(A) literal	(B) symbolic

This list is not intended to be a definitive test of any kind; it is merely an exercise to assist you in understanding the theory.*

Scoring Instructions Next to each answer there is a letter in parentheses (T F S or I). Put a mark in the scoring box below under the letter (T F S or I) that corresponds to your answer. After you have tallied your answers, add up the totals for each letter in the scoring box and enter the numerical total for each letter. For example, if your answer to question #1 is A, you would put a mark in box T.

The next step in scoring is to transfer your scores from the T, F, S, and I columns of the scoring box to the function compass below (Figure 5). First, check to see if you have scored it correctly by adding the T and F scores together, as well as the S and I scores. T + F should equal 6. The same is true for S + I; they equal 6.

	T	F	S	I
TOTALS				

ANSWER KEY

1.	A (T)	B (F)	7.	A (T)	B (F)
2.	A (I)	B (S)	8.	A (S)	B (I)
3.	A (S)	B (I)	9.	A (S)	B (I)
4.	A (T)	B (F)	10.	A (T)	B (F)
5.	A (T)	B (F)	11.	A (T)	B (F)
6.	A (S)	B (I)	12.	A (S)	B (I)

* There are a number of testing devices available that have creative applications and have been carefully developed over a number of years. The dangers of testing are considerable, and the instruments are often misused by persons who have no real appreciation for what vision is behind them. With this caveat stated, there are good reasons for continuing to develop these devices, which aid in communicating the necessary vision. *The Myers-Briggs Type Indicator* has been carefully researched and developed over many years and is recommended. For excellent materials on the Myer-Briggs Indicator, write to Consulting Psychologists Press, Inc., 577 College Avenue, Palo Alto, CA 94306.

T and F are a pair of opposites; S and I are also opposite pairs. Start by taking your highest score on each pair of opposites and circling the appropriate number on the top of the compass. If, for example, you scored 4 for T, mark one of the fours on the top of the compass and designate this *T*. Then draw a diameter to the 2 on the other side of the compass and designate this *F*. Do the same for your S and I scores. The following example illustrates the compass of a person who scored 4 for T, thus 2 for F; and 4 for S, thus 2 for I.

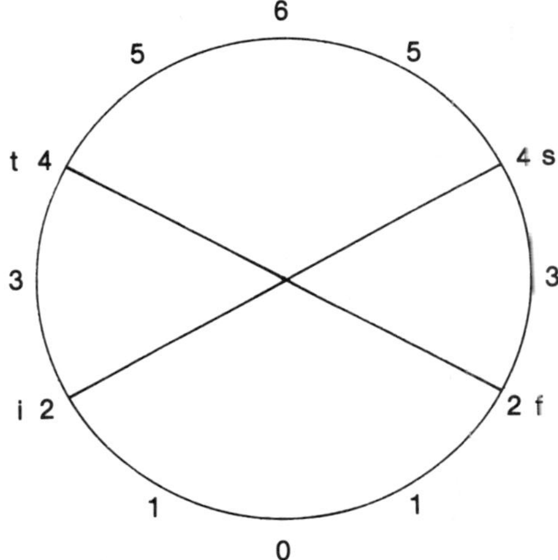

Now add up your scores and use Figure 5 to map out your own personal function compass.

FIGURE 5 Personal Function Compass.

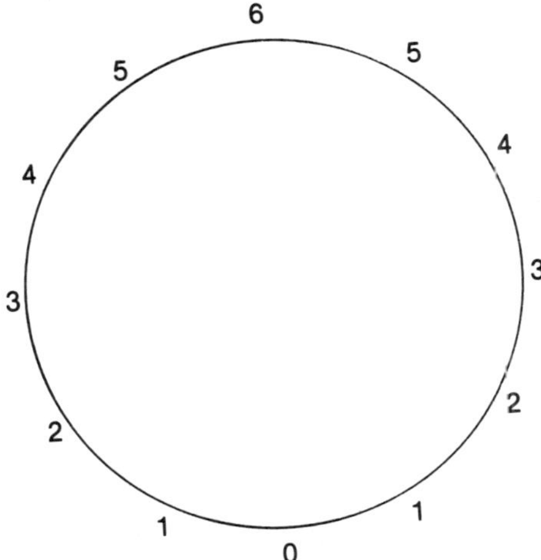

You now have the beginning of a compass to your personal *style.* We will explain its meaning shortly.

PERSONALITY FUNCTIONS AND STYLES

At the beginning of the development of depth psychology, there were significant clashes of personality. A study of these conflicts reveals a great deal about personality differences. When Carl Jung broke away from his mentor Sigmund Freud, he experienced a major rupture in his career. In order to understand what happened in this break-up and more clearly define his own directions, Jung spent a number of years creating his study of Psychological Types.* Jung's study was based on years of detailed observation of how different personalities function. Observation remains the best, most trustworthy method for making judgments within the system he created. At the start of creating a method for mapping out how you function which is based on Jung's work, and before we begin, a word of caution must be said. There are no quick and easy ways to make judgments about how you function. The purpose in presenting this method is not to make boxes to trap you in, but to enhance your ability to get free of them. It is best seen as a way of thinking about your functioning that is based on a profound awareness of the play of opposites within the whole of your personality. The development of a direct, personal awareness of what you have systematically excluded in your functioning is a major step toward real future growth. What will be presented here is a tool to aid you in creating this kind of awareness. Such approaches are really ancient tools. People have always been interested in creating effective methods for understanding differences within the larger whole.

In creating his method, Jung began by observing differences in how energy flows. Does your energy flow immediately outward or is it habitually directed inward toward a world of concepts and ideas? The manner in which your energy flows is called the basic *attitude* of your personality. It's how you stand *in* the world. These two basic attitudes are *introversion* and *extroversion.* The introvert's energy goes inward,

* C. G. Jung, *Psychological Types,* Collected Works, Vol. 6, Bollingen Series XX, Princeton University Press, 1971.

whereas the extrovert's tends outward toward action and expression. In planning your next career step, it is important to honor the fundamental attitude of your personality.

Now that we have established an understanding of your basic attitude, let's consider just how you function. We are concerned here with two fundamental ways of relating to your world. First we want to know the basic preference you have for taking the world in, that is, receiving information. Then we are concerned with how you prefer to process that information.

The two basic preferences for receiving information are called functions of *perception.* They are *sensation* and *intuition.* The basic preferences for processing information are called functions of *judgment.* They are *thinking* and *feeling.* Even though you function by way of your senses as well as your intuition, the nature of development is such that in general you neglect or exclude one of these modes of perceiving. Another way to put this is that you prefer one way of perceiving over the other and thus devote your attention and energy to the preferred mode. Knowing your preference can greatly assist career planning.

If you habitually perceive the world through your senses, you will be a keen observer of here-and-now facts and very attentive to details. Accountants and bookkeepers tend to have highly developed sensing functions. What is here and now present to the five senses is of greatest importance to those who prefer to perceive by way of sensation. Ideas and possibilities are thus much less compelling than they would be to someone who uses intuition more. The sensation function has a *present* time focus.

When you perceive primarily through intuition, the associations and possibilities that arise out of your own mind as a result of what you see take on more importance than actualities. This is the function that dreams. You are always running ahead of the situation being perceived as a result of your intuition. Intuition has a *future* time focus. Thus, you see that differences begin to develop as a result of depending on one mode of perception over the other.

After you take in information, you make judgments about it. You prefer to make judgments by way of either your *thinking or feeling* function. As is the case with sensation and intuition, thinking and feeling are opposites as functions of judgment.

The *thinking function* makes judgments that are logical, objective, and impersonal. When thinking, we deal with facts as they are experienced here and now, not in reference to any past associations. There is a kind of cool detachment in thinking that can often be an asset on the job. Thinkers enjoy analysis and value fairness; they often conclude just what ought to be done in any situation.

The *feeling function* on the other hand is subjective and concerned with personal values. History is important when the feeling function takes over, and judgments are frequently determined by associations with past events. Relationships are given much weight by this function, and the feeling person will often decide what has to be done in a situation on the basis of awareness of others and their feelings. Whatever the feeling person does, it has to be meaningful.

Ideally the functions work together to balance our personality. The completion of our personality occurs when we strike the perfect balance. Of course, such completeness is the work of a lifetime, but balance is an extremely important concept when it comes to planning your career. Success in any endeavor demands that you strike a minimal balance in your life.

Having examined these specific preferences, we want to bring them together in order to describe your personality *type* as that relates to career planning.*

By selecting your two preferred functions it is possible to group them in the following manner as represented in Figure 6.

By grouping the functions in this manner it is possible to identify four *basic styles* of functioning, represented in Figure 6. These styles, named Structural, Oceanic, Ethereal, and Experial result from a combination of two functions: one judging, and one perception. When the functions are grouped in this way, they provide a powerful tool for thinking about how different personalities make their world.

In Figure 7 we have transferred these styles of functioning to a circle which we designate the Style Compass.

Return again to Figure 5 and translate the scores from your personal compass to Figure 8 (page 22). Begin by identifying your two preferred functions, that is, your two highest scores. In the illustration case shown in the example before Figure 5, the preferred functions, T and S, were both 4 and thus equal in strength. In translating this to the Personal Style Compass, you would mark point I where T and S are equal in strength. If your T score was higher than your S score, for example, then you would mark the T/S point of the compass in

* Throughout this chapter we are indebted to the article by Humphrey Osmond, Miriam Siegler, and Richard Smoke. "Typology Revisited: A New Perspective," in *Psychological Perspectives,* Vol. 8, No. 2, Fall 1977, 206–219. Used by permission of *Psychological Perspectives.*

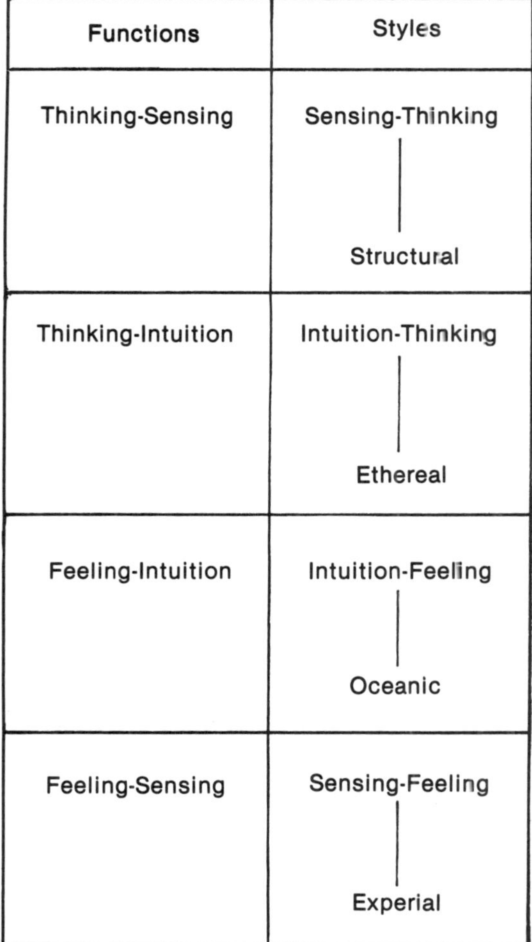

FIGURE 6 Grouping the Functions to Create Four Basic Styles.

Figure 8. If your S score was higher than your T then you would mark the S/T point and so forth. If in taking the instrument you scored 3 and 3 on a pair of opposites, the instrument has not helped you distinguish a preference. Theoretically the higher the scores on any function (T, F, S, or I) the more you prefer that function.

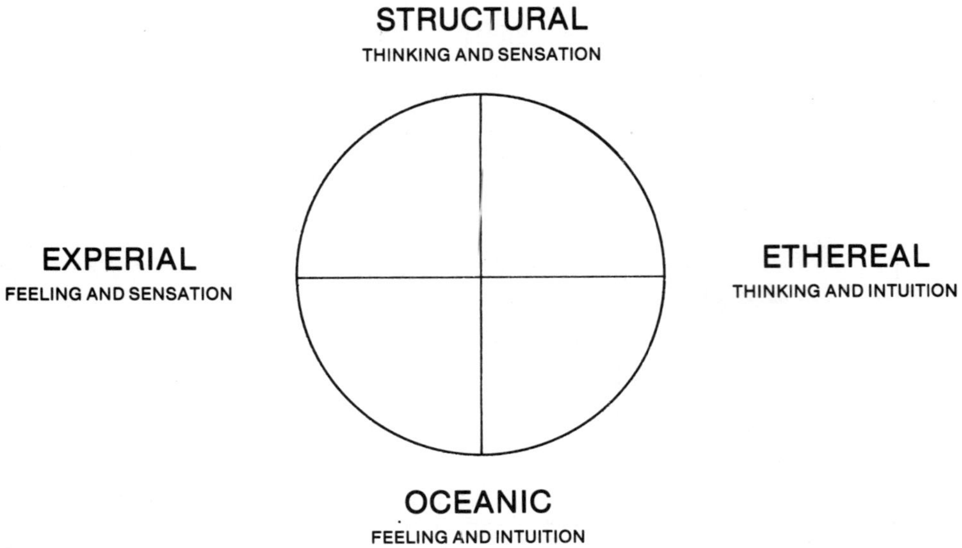

STRUCTURAL
THINKING AND SENSATION

EXPERIAL
FEELING AND SENSATION

ETHEREAL
THINKING AND INTUITION

OCEANIC
FEELING AND INTUITION

FIGURE 7 The Style Compass.

FIGURE 8 The Personal Style Compass.

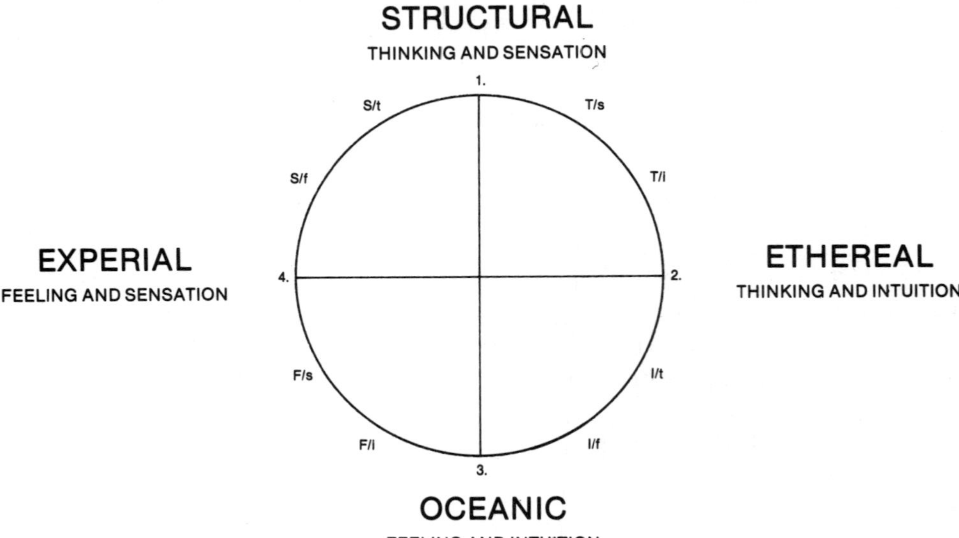

It is important to note that you are identifying a point or range on what we are calling your Personal Style Compass. In any circle there are an infinite number of points. There are therefore infinite nuances in such a method sufficient to embrace your unique personal style. What we will describe shortly are four points (1, 2, 3, and 4) on this circle, which we have named Structural, Oceanic, Ethereal, and Experial.

Each of these four broad styles represents the way in which people habitually make the world. By understanding each of these and exactly how they operate, you can begin to develop an awareness of your own functional style, of where you personally fit on such a compass and therefore how to best use your strengths and weaknesses in designing your career. You also can begin to see what you exclude, the natural prison of any style and what you must do to relate more to the whole. When a Mr. Inside in a work situation can truly appreciate the contribution of a Mr. Outside, there is an effective team. The frequent lack of appreciation of differences and resulting internal conflict that plagues organizations are functions of individuals who have no sense of the whole of themselves. Unless you begin dialogue with the excluded part, you cannot meet that part comfortably outside yourself. This is at the heart of most conflict between persons, as well as the source of numerous problems within organizations. Let's take a detailed look at the four styles of functioning.

THE FOUR STYLES OF FUNCTIONING

The Structural Style

The combination of thinking and sensation creates the world of the Structural. In some ways the law of Structurals is "What I can't quantify, I can't manage." The split between your subjective side and your objective side is significant if this is your style. You may find anything subjective and unable to be nailed down to facts a disruption. The creation of systems, long-range plans, maps, and theories would come easily to you. Psychologist Edward L. Thorndike is often quoted as saying "If I can't measure it, it doesn't exist." There is great power and efficiency in such a position, and the control which it creates can produce a great deal. The genius of American organizational ability in many ways stems from the power and discipline of the Structural approach to reality. Servan-Schreiber's book *The American Challenge* is the result of an outsider, a man of another culture, another style, looking at America's management genius and the challenge it presents to the European community.*

* Jean Servan-Schreiber, *The American Challenge* (New York: Atheneum, 1979).

The book is a good example of how one style can see the merits of another, though the view tends to be either overly positive or excessively negative. One style viewing the opposite tends to either romanticize or caricature what is seen. The predominance of the sensation and thinking functions in organizations in the United States is a major key to their successes. If you are Structural in style, your limits will also indicate what you must do to further develop.

In Figure 9, which describes the Structural style and lists some examples of personalities that seem to embody these characteristics, are two sections headed "As perceived by others" and "As perceiving others." Under each of these headings are signs indicating positive (+) and negative (−) perceptions. The "As perceived" section lists adjectives that would be used by someone looking at the Structural and describing what they saw either positively or negatively. Servan-Schreiber saw order, reason, dependability, skill, and responsibility in the genius of American management. Critics of the Structural style see it as dry, lifeless, rigid, domineering, and tyrannical. Under "As perceiving others" are adjectives a Structural would use when describing others, specifically their opposite. As a Structural you may be capable of seeing in your opposite what you need but don't have—warmth, spontaneity, flexibility, and

FIGURE 9 Structural Style.

Characteristics

- Split between subjective and objective
- Subjective intrudes, disrupts
- Make structures: Maps, systems, plans, theories
- Paint into corners, creates binds

Examples

Florence Nightingale	Richard Nixon
Aristotle	Lady Macbeth
Queen Elizabeth I	Malcolm X

As perceived by others:

+	−
Orderly	Dry
Reasonable	Lifeless
Dependable	Rigid
Skillful	Domineering
Responsible	Tyrannical

As perceiving others:

+	−
Warm	Sloppy
Spontaneous	Unprincipled
Flexible	Can't face facts
Imaginative	Ineffectual

(the major direction for development for structurals)

imagination. On the other hand, if you perceive your opposite negatively, you are more inclined to caricature and you'll see a sloppy, unprincipled, ineffectual person who can't face facts.

STRUCTURAL WORK STYLE

As a Structural, you are quite dependable and often, at your best, an adaptable realist. You have a practical respect for facts which you know, remember, and use in an effortless manner. Any work that demands careful attention to facts and details, such as administration or maintenance of an organization, is well suited to your style. Having a highly developed sensing function, you are often at ease with mathematical manipulations like accounting or bookkeeping, as well as the logistical aspects of work like scheduling and procedures. In artistic endeavors you will be a real craftsman, at ease with detailed reproductions. Abstract art, on the other hand, may be more difficult due to your underdeveloped intuition.

With a developed thinking function you naturally objectify the world and consequently your subjective side is not readily accessible. You may find it difficult to sympathize with other people's point of view. You learn more from direct experience than from books. You have respect for orderly efficiency and conduct your affairs in this manner, expecting others to do the same. Your developmental needs are directly related to opening yourself to your functions of feeling and intuition. The expansion of empathic capacities, and the development of the creative imagination are at the heart of your future development. Be open to other points of view. Listen and appreciate others in order to expand your capacity for empathy. Stretch your imagination, let yourself dream a little.

If you are Structural, you function in the world by way of Thinking and Sensation. You exclude the subjective in a systematic way and this creates your own prison. Every style is its own prison. To the extent that you can see the limits of how you systematically make the world, to that extent you can appreciate the whole and break free of the limitations of your style. This will be the beginning of your real development and crucial to significant career development.

Since Structurals function primarily by way of thinking and sensing, they possess great power in effective, precise, organizing abilities. Their ease in objectifying the world enables them to be cool under pressure. They are not convinced of anything except by reasoning. Western organizations have been dominated by Structurals. The rapid growth of American business is due in large measure to a Structural orientation. All of us enjoy today the fruits of this endeavor: an orderly, structured, efficiently run society.

The Oceanic Style

Opposite the Structural is the Oceanic. The functions of feeling and intuition which the Structural has excluded are relied upon by the Oceanic. Critics of modern Western culture and its emphasis on science, of the Western mind set generally, all include the neglect of those realities most central to the Oceanic personality.* If you are this style, the way in which you experience the world runs counter to the determining forces of Western society. In the sixties, the explosive reactions against Western institutions that were exhibited throughout the world were based upon the re-emphasizing of feeling and intuition as authentic modes of experience. The imbalance of the Structural apart from the Oceanic became a global social issue during this decade. Countercultural movements surfaced which are going to be increasingly influential on personal and organizational life in the future. Career directions and planning are significantly influenced by these counter trends in the culture, since they have so much to do with value issues.

The model we are developing has been primarily a tool for considering how the individual functions and grows toward his own wholeness or completion. In the above remarks we are using it to consider how the society is struggling toward a balance or completion also. Today's culture needs to integrate the Oceanic.

You, the Oceanic, are especially concerned with values. What for most people are impersonal realities tend to become subjective and personal for you. The strength of the intuitive function often makes you appear mystical in nature. Seen negatively, this tendency is judged to create helplessness or disruptive behavior. The frequently intense reactions of the business community against the countercultural youth groups can be better understood in light of the difference which exists between these two worlds.

On the other hand, the abhorrence for structure which characterizes you as an Oceanic can create havoc if carried to extremes. Mao Tse-tung is frequently quoted as calling for "Chaos, more chaos" in his effort to keep organization from freezing into inefficient bureaucracy. Recent events in China can be viewed as the balancing effort needed to restore order in a country paralyzed by the chaos of conflicting, anarchic groups. Without doubt, most organizations in the West could benefit from more creative chaos stemming from an appreciation for what the Oceanic sees and experiences. Feeling and intuition are the most neglected functions in Western organizational life. They are the Oceanic

* Houston Smith, "Excluded Knowledge: A Critique of the Modern Western Mind Set," *Teachers College Record,* Vol. 80, Number 3.

Characteristics

- Life is seamless whole
- Subjectifying of impersonal
- Dreamy, moody
- Flexibility - bend not break
- Great capacity for input
"Chaos more chaos."

Examples

Joan of Arc	Isadora Duncan
Churchill	Gandhi

As perceived by others:

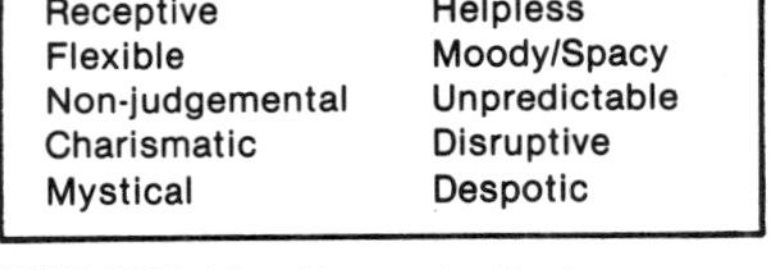

+	—
Receptive	Helpless
Flexible	Moody/Spacy
Non-judgemental	Unpredictable
Charismatic	Disruptive
Mystical	Despotic

As perceiving others:

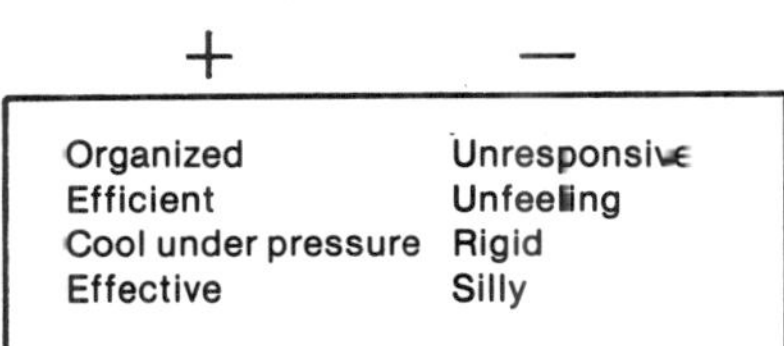

+	—
Organized	Unresponsive
Efficient	Unfeeling
Cool under pressure	Rigid
Effective	Silly

FIGURE 10 Oceanic Style.

gift. Mid-career shifts often result when persons realize a strong need to express more of their feeling and intuitive side, and find it difficult or impossible to do in their organizational setting. Later, in a separate section in this chapter on mid-career development, this issue will be examined in detail.

Your great strength as an Oceanic is your ability to see the large picture—*i.e.,* to take in the world as a whole. You are flexible, especially with abstract ideas, and have an ability to take in large quantities of information. Having developed the feeling function, you are very concerned with values and the meaning of life. Work for you must have meaning, no matter how much money you make. Frequently money is secondary, and getting rich seldom serves to motivate you. Figure 10 describes the characteristics of an Oceanic.

OCEANIC WORK STYLE

You have a great curiosity for new ideas, and are, at your best, capable of long-range vision. Your inner ideals tend to govern your life and you must believe in what you do to be effective. Since you are concerned with people and the common good, you tend to be impatient with indifference. You will be best at work which enables you to deal directly with people and in an endeavor having social significance.

Your difficulty is that detail and routine unconnected to any significant project bores you. This results from your insufficiently developed sensing function. Having a highly developed feeling function enables you to be very understanding of others. Compassion is easy, but so is intolerance.

When you find a work that you *believe in* you will be highly productive in whatever field. Never accept work which conflicts with your values.

You need to learn to distance yourself from situations which you too readily personalize. You also need to continually check out your inspirations to make sure they are grounded in reality. Learn to objectify rather than personalize experiences. Develop a tougher skin, to protect yourself. Develop more political sense and continually test your ideas with very pragmatic realists.

Your qualities as an Oceanic are interesting to consider in relation to current events in the world that are influencing economies and job possibilities. Your ability to see life as a seamless whole would appear to be an almost necessary quality in any leader or manager these days. The conflict of many countries with OPEC stems from the failure of world governments to cooperate and understand the distribution of energy resources around the globe. OPEC insists it is concerned with creating Third World solidarity. The United States feels, as our leaders say, that OPEC has a knife at its neck. The sense of the whole seems lacking here. This global conflict will be one of the major forces influencing careers over the next decade. Those who can see through and beyond the dynamics at play in these conflicting forces will be able to plan their own lives effectively, and prepare themselves for leadership roles in the future.

A comment might be made here about the functions that are primary to the Oceanic and their relation to men and women in the culture. By and large, the feeling and intuitive functions are relegated to women. Men therefore, because of cultural pressures, tend to neglect these functions. The woman who is career-oriented is thus up against organizational environments dominated by men who function in a manner which excludes feeling and intuition. The contribution the professional woman can make in such a situation is evident, in light of the type of prison or imbalance that now exists. For men who are Oceanic, the challenge is likewise significant. England needed the charisma and vision of Winston Churchill in its crisis during World War II. A global crisis is emerging connected with energy and the needs of the planetary whole which will require comparable moral leadership and vision. Oceanic qualities built into your personal development can enable you to respond to the organizational needs now surfacing.

The Ethereal Style

If you are Ethereal you rely upon the functions of thinking and intuition. In doing so you can often be a bridging or mediating influence in the conflicts described so far that occur between Structurals and Oceanics. The thinking function's stength enables you to relate the Structural's emphasis on logic and rationality, while your intuition enables you to see the possibilies envisioned by the Oceanic. This bridging capacity is likely to be needed more and more in organizational settings where value conflicts intensify. As an Ethereal, you are the visionary, the innovator. You are constantly seeing new possibilities, new things to be done. Your imagination is highly developed and you have great confidence in your inspirations—they guide your life.

Your limitations could be expressed in your inability to attend to the routine and detail of life, or in an inability to understand other people's point of view. By dialoging with your neglected side of sensing and feeling, you develop yourself and will be capable of the great mediating work of the decade ahead. Appreciation, empathy, and stability are capacities you should struggle to develop.

The characteristics of the Ethereal style contained in Figure 11 are well suited to developing ways to address the larger issues of the eighties. The focus on what is real is so fundamental that the important questions can be raised. The weaknesses of the Ethereal should likewise be kept in mind. Like any style left alone, the Ethereal can get so caught up in his vision that he is seen as a kook, hopelessly indecisive and remote. Biographical studies of the persons listed in the chart can add to your appreciation of this type.

ETHEREAL WORK STYLE

As an Ethereal in style you are the innovator, always seeing new possibilities or finding new ways of doing things. You are very creative, an effective and inventive problem-solver. In general, you are very independent, bordering on individualistic. You will excel at work calling for reorganizing skills, design abilities, project promotion, or planning.

A major difficulty arises for you in dealing with humdrum detail. Work that enables you to be involved in a series of projects is most appropriate. Your major contribution will be in designing such projects and getting them launched. You generally prefer that following through to completion be done by others.

As an Ethereal you need to develop your sensing and feeling functions. It is very important for you to attend to the feelings of other people as well as to the concrete facts which characterize your work situation. Talk over your ideas with an Experial. Come to appreciate the limits of your inspirations by carefully listening to others.

Carl Jung, on whose work this method rests, was an Ethereal. He constitutes a bridge of enormous importance between the Western mind and the ancient wisdom of the East. His life and work begin to present in significant detail what is involved in the effort to live the whole, rather than be satisfied with the functions of only half. Jung's break with Freud, already mentioned, threw him into a major life crisis out of which came his most important works. The perspective contained in his work throws more light on the possibilities of growth in adult life than can be found in most academic psychology, whose focus has been on behavior of animals or pathology. It has application to our developmental stages as well as to the development of organizations. In the comments made so far concerning the neglected functions of organizations are beginning

FIGURE 11 Ethereal Style.

Characteristics

- Psyche is real - mind is limitless
- Images, ideas, theories are primary
- Often concerned about what is real
  "Details delight me. Ramifications enchant me."
  Sayers' Lord Peter Wimsey

Examples

Einstein	Martin Luther King
Darwin	Karl Marx
Virginia Woolf	Ben Franklin

As perceived by others:

+	−
Verbally adroit	Kooky
Witty	Indecisive
Imaginative	Remote
Playful	"Spacy"
Visionary	Unfeeling

As perceiving others:

+	−
Earthy	Boring
Practical	Unimaginative
Warm	Flakey
Open	Inarticulate

attempts at analyzing the developmental needs of those organizations which contain the work life of most people. In the past, the growth of these organizations has been at the expense of what is described here as the Oceanic. The exclusion of the Oceanic was not conscious, or intentional. Rather, it was the natural path of development. A kind of law was being followed. But now this law must change as a new stage of growth is reached. What was true and effective as a law early on can no longer be followed. Jung states it well in describing the development of the individual: "But we cannot live the afternoon of life according to the program of life's morning—for what was great in the morning will be little at evening, and what in the morning was true will at evening have become a lie."* Western society is at this kind of turning point in its development; so too is the corporation. Its balance and wholeness will be enhanced it if can open itself to the Oceanic perspective—the sensitivity to values, the subjective, the person, the planet as a whole. Lest all this be too easily dismissed it should be mentioned that the consideration of the neglected half is *necessary* to development. Not to consider the excluded part is to succumb to the mere biological forces of decay that take the human organism into old age. Practically speaking, it appears to be in the enlightened self-interest of all organizations to consider their relation to the whole and to do this in two ways. There is, first, the whole of the organization itself and its excluded functions. Then there is the planetary whole and the role of the organization in relating to the globe. OPEC and the Third World generally might be better understood in this context. It is simply not enough to say, "Nuts to OPEC" or to mount a "moral equivalent of war" against a hostile cartel. Deeper issues are involved in the present and leaders are needed who see more deeply.

The Ethereal vision of Jung and the tool of this method might be a contribution to the development of the needed leadership. In planning your career you cannot ignore these larger issues so central to the approach of the 1980s.

The Experial Style

If you are opposite the Ethereal, you are the Experial in style, which means you deal with the world through feeling and sensation. Archie Bunker for whom reality is concrete, direct and personal, is Experial. His concern for values is evident and often appears as mere bigotry or stubbornness. Figure 12 describes the Experial style. What Archie

* C. G. Jung, *Modern Man in Search of A Soul* (New York: Harcourt Brace, 1933).

Characteristics

- Reality is concrete, direct, personal
- Ease in relating, responding
- Here-now orientation
- Social glue, moral exemplars

Examples

Harry Truman	Scarlet O'Hara
Eleanor Roosevelt	Marlon Brando
Konrad Lorenz	King Lear

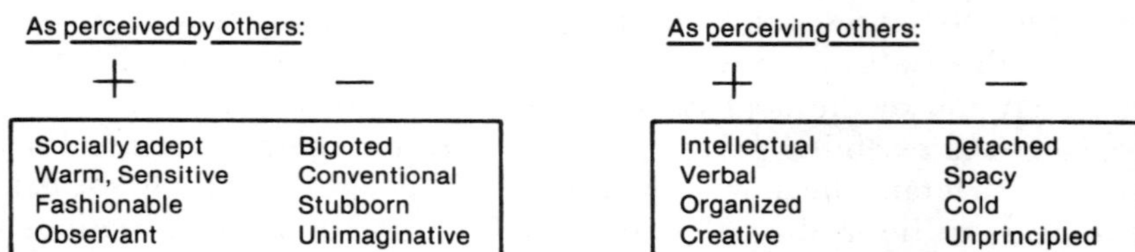

As perceived by others:

+	−
Socially adept	Bigoted
Warm, Sensitive	Conventional
Fashionable	Stubborn
Observant	Unimaginative

As perceiving others:

+	−
Intellectual	Detached
Verbal	Spacy
Organized	Cold
Creative	Unprincipled

FIGURE 12 Experial Style.

complains about in "Meathead," his son-in-law, is exactly what he has neglected in his own development. The highflown ideas of "Meathead" would go a long way in allowing Archie to grow as an adult. Much of the success of this TV series can be attributed to its artful inclusion of the whole within its dramatizations. Like any work of art the interplay of all the styles is present.

In a recent seminar for corporate level managers from IBM, the style compass was being discussed as a tool for management development. One of the women managers present in the seminar who considered herself to be an Ethereal was complaining about a young man on her staff. She saw this person as an Experial, and was frustrated at her inability to "Get him to see the big picture." Experials tend to blank out, become glassy eyed when it comes to the big picture. At the same time, this manager could see the fellow's good qualities—everyone liked him, he was a cohesive element in her department, bringing people together. The lesson here for these opposite styles involves not expecting what is impossible in a person, who habitually leaves out a part of reality. Not that growth is impossible, but the time may not be appropriate for an individual to begin looking at his neglected functions.

Only after consolidating one's style in the first part of life is there the readiness to begin the effort to open up to the ignored functions. It is important not to rush this readiness, and in the meantime, learn to value what is present in the world even though different from your own style.

For young people graduating from college, defining your functional preferences will be your major focus for the next fifteen years. The choice of work upon graduation will have a major impact on your personal definition and should therefore be done with care. Your life experiences thus far should give you a sense of your initial functional preferences. The principle of work choice would be to select a job which helps you consolidate these preferences. At the middle of your life, shifts will be necessary; we will speak of this later in the chapter.

EXPERIAL WORK STYLE

As an Experial you are a friendly, good-natured realist. You are at ease socially and therefore good at work demanding interaction with people. Good sales personnel are frequently Experials. You like things kept simple and on a factual basis. Philosophers bore you. You are very observant, knowing precisely what's happening in social situations. Frequently you have a great love for nature and you may have artistic taste. You will enjoy any work that requires tact or sympathy for people: sales, social work, veterinarian, etc.

Your difficulty is that you may become too earthbound, with no vision of what's possible. You may also be a poor disciplinarian, with others as well as yourself. You need to develop your intuition and thinking functions. Big ideas are important for you, even though you find them difficult.

Avoid oversociability on the job and narrow-minded gossiping. Develop a broader picture of the world through literature and art.

PERFORMANCE APPRAISAL SYSTEMS AND THE STYLE COMPASS

Using the style categories can also be a method of assessing your past career performance. A personal appraisal system can be set up whereby your weaknesses or problem areas might be explained and better understood when seen as a function of the limits of a particular style. Performance appraisal systems in organizational settings could also employ this method in order to add depth to their evaluations. Currently, most of these systems are too numbers-oriented and fail to provide direction for development.

It is possible, using the methods that are presented here, to establish a performance appraisal system based on the requirements of adult development. Management development programs generally can benefit from this approach, which relates personal development to career development. The weaknesses of performance appraisal systems are becoming more apparent and the complaint about managers never giving honest feedback to their employees is rampant. Without a context in which to make judgments about what an individual needs to do to improve himself, people will continue to write meaningless or innocuous entries on appraisal forms. Careful use of a method that considers the development of the whole person in work situations can begin to correct these weaknesses. Such a method also goes beyond the mere manipulation of persons to make them feel better in basically bad situations. Because it addresses the play of opposites in the context of the whole, it also relates to improving the system in which work takes place.

MID-CAREER SHIFTS

There are a number of principles of development that should guide career planning during the mid-life period. By understanding your personal style, especially in relation to your opposite which embodies your neglected side, your career planning can be connected to your personal development task.

The first principle regarding your career development is:

1. *Build on the positive aspects of your style, but develop in the direction of your neglected side.*

Another way to state this is choose a work which utilizes your strengths, but calls you in the direction of your limitations.

Next, the intense pressures from within that are frequently related to the demands of the neglected functions need to be carefully examined. A common early response is to identify with these new urges and be tempted to abandon one's past entirely. This calls for the stating of a second principle:

2. *Whenever possible, maintain continuity with the past. Discontinuities that are the result of flipping over into one's opposite are dangerous and usually counterproductive.*

Radical career shifts are rare. It is possible to involve neglected functions in gradual ways that meaningfully change the experience of a specific job and renew a career. Frequently changing the context in which one functions, but building on the functions where there is experience and strength, is the best way to make a shift.

A third principle, which has been implied throughout this chapter, can be stated explicitly in this way:

3. *Mid-career shifts will be satisfying only when they relate to a self-created sense of vocation. A sense of vocation is the result of seeing the part one plays in relation to the whole—increasingly this involves the planetary whole.*

Throughout his writings that relate to adult development issues, Jung stresses the need to create a sense of the ultimate meaning of personal life. This is a central requirement for adult development and applies directly to one's work. When life task and one's work can be related, there is a significant release of creative energy—a release worth struggling for.

Struggle is part of a fourth principle:

4. *At mid-life, career change and personal change are intertwined. Because they cannot be separated, the changes involve struggle and a great deal of hard work.*

The romanticization of career change characteristic of some journalistic coverage of the phenomenon usually ignores the dimension of struggle. Just pack it all in and live happily ever after in New Hampshire, Florida, Oregon, etc., is the apparent message. But lately, contradictory messages are coming in from New Hampshire, Florida, etc. on how hard it is. For many, such moves prove to be only temporary.

When Jung was about to make his real break from Freud, he was involved in writing the work which began to make public his theoretical differences with his mentor. The crucial chapter in that work, which he could not write until he made the final decision to go his own way, is entitled "The Sacrifice" in the English edition.* Such is the nature of a fifth principle:

5. *Significant career change involves real personal sacrifice. When one moves into genuinely new dimensions of functioning, much of the old must be given up, and the giving up is experienced as sacrifice.*

The period of the middle of life is frequently talked about these days in terms of the crisis it involves. The emphasis in the five principles

* C. G. Jung, *Symbols of Transformation,* Collected Works, Volume 5, Chapter VIII.

stated here is on the requirements for significant growth during this period—they do involve struggle, sacrifice, commitment, and the desire to create a sense of vocation or ultimate meaning in one's life and work. Perhaps these realities present the individual with a feeling of crisis because they are uncommon, relatively new concerns. The decade of the 1980s is certain to require that these qualities be more and more present in individuals, if there is to be comparable quality in the various environments that make up the culture as a whole. Certainly, the work environments are presently crying out for more quality and they promise to demand even more in the future with major global economic changes in the picture. Mid-career shifts may become increasingly necessary for growing numbers of people. The effort in this chapter has been to provide some tools for making this necessity a real opportunity for growth. The middle of life can be as intensely developmental as the adolescent period, and career development can be made a part of that growth. When this is the case both individuals and organizations benefit.

SUMMARY

This chapter began with Heraclitus and a statement of purposes. The epigram about the way up being the way down embodies the unity of opposites within the whole that might be clearer now in light of the method for considering opposites presented here. The method enables you to see how you function in relation to the whole. This kind of insight gives you an appreciation of the opposites within, making understanding of opposite styles a possibility. It also provides you some understanding of what you have neglected so far in your own development, so that you can discover the direction of your growth. A basic theme of this chapter was to relate your career development to these fundamental requirements of your personal development.

Throughout the chapter the perspective was a depth one, that is, looking at the levels of functioning that complement the behavioral viewpoint. This is the level which is most tied up with culture and the value shifts that take place there. Because of the significant cultural upheavals occurring at this moment in history, this perspective is essential in considering career and career shifts. The inner world of values and beliefs for many people is in the kind of turmoil that makes career choices necessarily involved with value issues. Skill identification is necessary but insufficient in enabling you to truly know what you want. The perspective on career development offered here is presented as a complementary viewpoint in an effort to assist you in career choices.

Another theme which has been presented here has to do with making career choices in the context of current global needs. If the seventies focused on the self, the following years call for similar concern with the planet as a whole. Believing in your work demands that you see it in relation to the whole. The world situation requires that all of us find ways of seeing our part as cathedral building and not an alienated carrying of rocks. The style compass does offer a way of considering the large global issues as conflicting opposites within a whole that is struggling to develop itself. What the West has systematically left out of its focus in the last few centuries is available in the ancient wisdoms of the East. What the East has neglected in its own history can be gotten from the West. It is possible to relate your personal career choices to this global urge for completion and wholeness. Doing so makes a sense of vocation possible and restores quality to one's working life. In the future, leadership in organizational life will come from individuals who have such a sense. If these kinds of considerations help you inform your career choices, they will ensure genuine renewal and long-term career satisfaction. The special needs of mid-career change were addressed in the formulation of the five principles.

From this general model of how you function, we move to a general model of how organizations function. This is the subject of Chapter 3.

HOW ORGANIZATIONS FUNCTION AND WHERE YOU FIT

PURPOSE

The purpose of this chapter is to give you a method for understanding the whole of organizational life. A basic model of how organizations function will be presented which can be used in planning your personal career direction. Just as the last chapter discussed career in the larger framework of personal development and global issues, this chapter will concentrate on situating your career direction within the total context of organizational functions.

If you are entering or reentering the employment system or are attempting a mid-career shift, you need to know how organizations operate. Without this knowledge it becomes impossible to make informed choices since you don't know your options. For example, persons who know they enjoy working with people often think of working in personnel, a name with which they are vaguely familiar. In testing their knowledge, we often discover they equate personnel with interviewing people for jobs. Since little else is known, their choices are diminished.

Similarly, if you are graduating from a university in a liberal arts program, you probably know little about modern business organizations. Stumbling into a job at this stage merely because one appears can set you on a path that holds little interest or meaning. Many of today's problems with decreasing productivity can be attributed to people choosing jobs which do not fit them. The lack of information on just how organizations work and on current developments in various industries is appalling.

College graduates are not alone in their lack of knowledge. Many people with extensive business experience who have worked exclusively in one function such as sales have practically no idea of what goes on in other areas of an organization in which they are working. Again, this lack of information limits career options. They feel forced to stay in sales whether they like it or not.

The single career imperative that has dominated cultural thinking is also a result of limited knowledge. Only recently have large organizations begun to address the question of making information available about career-paths, that is, describing the relationship between various work activities so as to create career development patterns and options. Such information would go a long way in expanding people's career choices.

By understanding how organizations function you can better design your career in terms of your own preferences.

SYSTEMS THEORY

Organizations are best understood from the point of view of systems theory, which explains the relationships of parts to the whole. An organization is a living entity or whole that consists of a complex system, or network, of interrelated parts.

Systems theory is used in a variety of disciplines. In ecology, for instance, the concept of an eco-system is an example of it. An eco-system is defined as a complex interrelationship of organisms within a given environment. Simply put, it explains that there is a very definite relationship between the smallest micro-organism in the soil of a forest, and the plant and animal life of that forest. Every aspect of the forest is connected to and interdependent with every other aspect.

In describing organizations as complex systems it is helpful to distinguish them from *industries* and *functions.* An industry is also a system consisting of interrelated organizations which are engaged in providing the same product or service, for example: automobile manufacturers, or steel makers. A *function* is the same work which is carried out in more than one industry. For example, marketing is a function; as such it is a work performed in organizations across all industries.

FUNCTIONS AND SERVICES

There are six basic parts to our model of organizations, each distinct yet interrelated. These parts are called functions. Within these functions all the work of the organization takes place. The functions are named: Personnel/Human Resources, Communications, Marketing, Finance, Research and Development, and Operations/Administration.

In addition to the six functions the model identifies three services: Information Systems, Legal, and Management. Information Systems and Legal are considered cross-functional components in that they serve each of the six functions. Management is a service rendered in the six basic functions as well as in the two cross-functional components. Figures 13 and 14 provide graphic illustrations of these relationships.

Take for example an organization within the book publishing industry. The primary purpose of this organization is to publish books. In order to achieve its purpose the organization must select written material, put this material in readable form, print the material, and get the finished product to readers who buy it. It must further maintain itself by organizing, rewarding, selecting and training its members, and at the end of all this pay its owners a profit for their investment.

The six functions of the model incorporate all of the work described above. Since the model is generic, the words used to describe these functions in the book publishing industry will be different from those used in another industry. Even within the same industry, words will differ from company to company, yet the work is functionally the same.

In the case of publishing, Research and Development is essentially concerned with acquiring new material to print and sell. Marketing is concerned with promoting and distributing the product to get the public to buy more books. Finance is concerned with maintaining positive balance sheets. Communications is concerned with improving relationships with book buyers, governments, and employees. Personnel/Human Resources attends to recruiting, training, and compensating employees. Operations/Administration concerns itself with editing and producing the company's products.

Frequently people just entering the employment system articulate their objective as "management." Such an objective is vague at best; it cannot be pursued unless it is linked to a specific organizational function or service area. A management position within marketing, for exam-

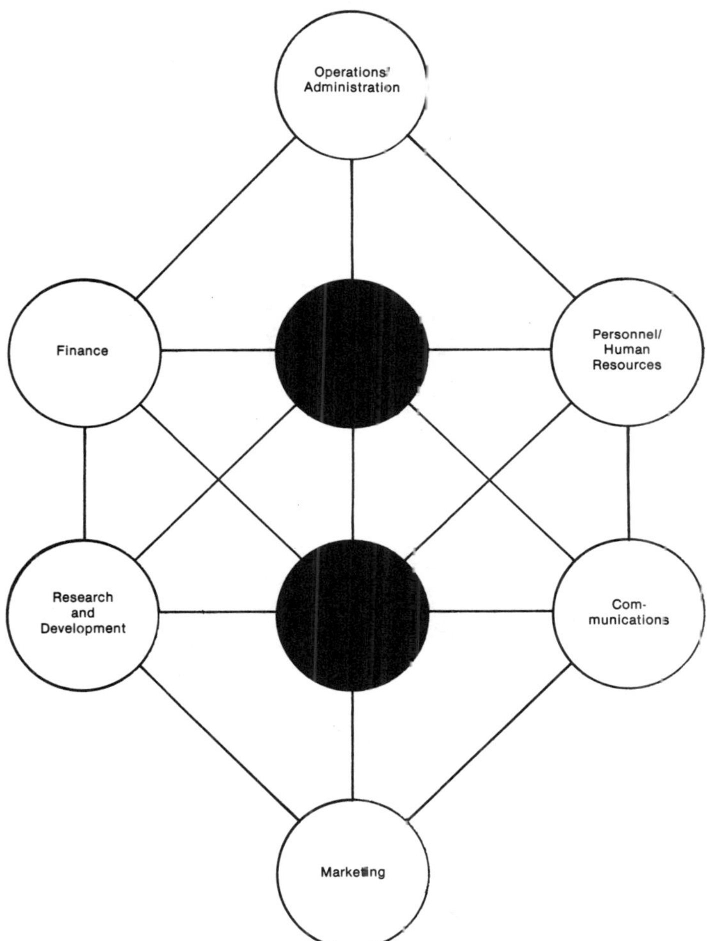

FIGURE 13 The Network of Functions Expressing the Work of the Organization.

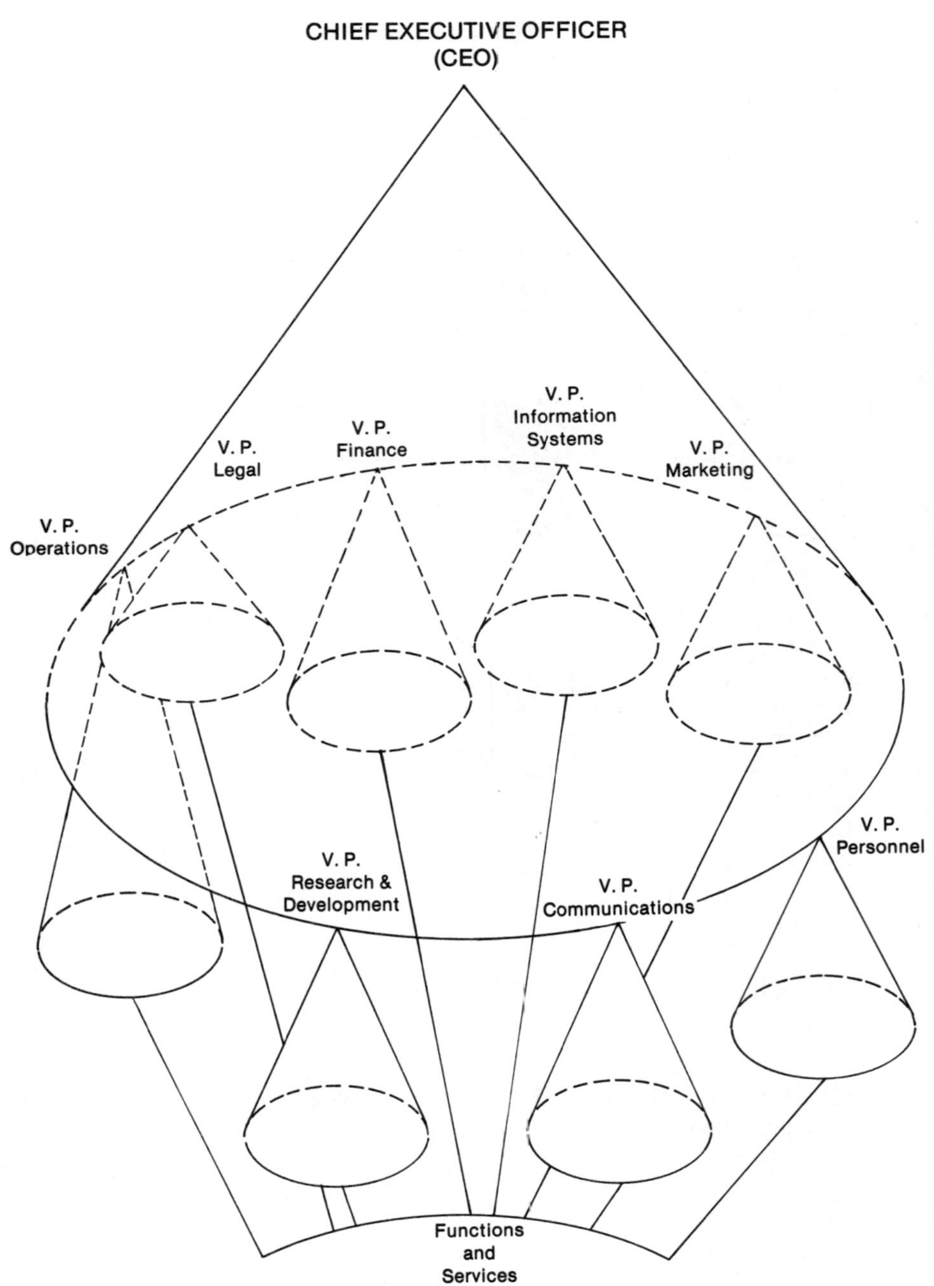

FIGURE 14 The Management of Functions and Services.

ple, begins to have meaning. So an early decision you must make in doing career planning involves determining in which part of the organization you wish to work. To make the decision you must become familiar with how each *part* operates. Such knowledge will enable you to begin to clearly state your objectives.

Deciding on the specific part of organizational life with which you want to be connected can't be over-emphasized. Consider Leo Wright, a client who came to us with over fifteen years of extensive business experience. He had been a senior vice-president in charge of corporate planning for two Fortune 500 companies. He had an MBA and DBA from Harvard with an emphasis on the marketing and finance functions. He was chief executive officer of a $500,000,000/year company in his last position, which he had left because of a merger. He thoroughly understood how organizations functioned, so lack of information was not his problem. Yet he had a major problem which he expressed in this way:

"I have extensive experience and knowledge of business, and yet because of my high level positions, I have become a generalist. I have no specific industry focus, and worse yet, I have no *functional focus.* Do I go after a position in marketing, or finance, or operations? What industry do I pursue? It's very confusing."

Since a first principle is to decide in what area you wish to work, and since functions and service areas occur in all organizations, this decision does not exclude any industry or any sector (private or public). Making this decision will help you focus, and bring you a step closer to being able to execute an effective job search.

If you find it difficult to articulate a functional focus, you may prefer to start with an industry focus. This particular difficulty often means you are interested in the *operations* functions of that industry. As you will see, operations defines the nature of each industry.

If you take a closer look at each function you see it includes a variety of activities. These activities are responsible for areas of work directly connected to the function's purposes.

For example, the human resource function is performed in all organizations regardless of size. In smaller organizations this function may be carried out informally by one person. As organizations get larger, the function gets more formalized with more staff to do the work. In large organizations, Human Resources has very defined activities.

You can now begin to see, from the variety of activities listed, that this function includes much more than interviewing people for jobs. In fact, many of the activities involve no direct work with people.

Of course, the model we have presented here is generic. When applied to specific organizations in specific industries, it will take slightly different shape. Words and titles change from one organization to the next. Depending on the industry, there will be greater emphasis on specific functions; certain activities will be placed under different functions, and so on. Despite these variations, all organizations attend to the work defined by these functions. As a job searcher you must understand the model in order to make decisions and know where you want to approach organizations. To deepen your understanding, each part of the model will be briefly described.

Personnel/Human Resources

Since World War II this function has changed dramatically. What was predominantly a purely clerical function has become a complex area dealing with the training and development of people and a good deal of government regulation. Figure 15 indicates this complexity.

The changes within this function have taken place gradually, described here in ten-year periods. For the ten years following the war (1945–1955), a number of activities such as compensation (wage and salary systems), recruitment, and systematized training efforts, became consolidated at the corporate level.

Phase two, from 1955–1965, saw the development of management training, organization and manpower planning, and employee communications.

Phase three (1965–1975), which continues today, stresses activities related to the planning and control of the organization's future in terms of people. Manpower planning, staffing, organization development, equal employment opportunity, and a renewed emphasis on safety and health dominate this latest phase.

The following activities constitute the work found in the Personnel/Human Resources function of most organizations. In large companies, each activity may involve an entire department.

Recruitment selecting and hiring new employees.

Compensation Administering wages and salaries.

Labor Relations Maintaining relationships with all groups that are or could become bargaining units.

Benefits Administrating all benefits for employees (e.g., vacation and insurance).

Safety and Health Assuring company compliance with safety and health legislation.

FIGURE 15 The Personnel Function in a Large Pharmaceutical Company, Corporate Personnel Relations Unit. From Report 712, *The Personnel Function: Changing Objectives and Organizations* (New York: The Conference Board, 1977), p. 69, by permission of The Conference Board.

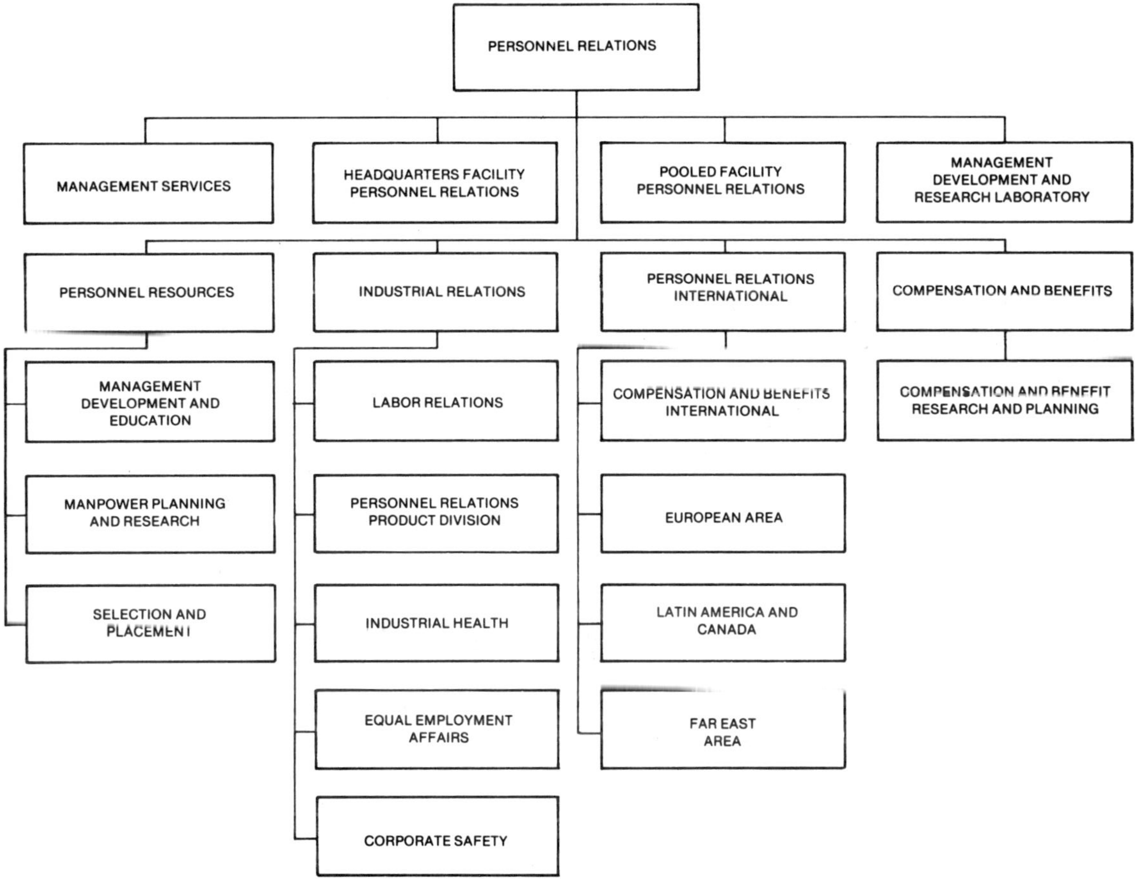

Equal Employment Opportunity (EEO) Assuring compliance with EEO legislation, and minority development.

Employee Communications Planning, preparing, and distributing publications for employees.

Organization Development Applying different behavioral science techniques to organizational life.

Training and Development Educating employees at all levels.

Manpower Planning Researching and planning future manpower needs while analyzing productivity issues.

Thinking of personnel as a work directly involved with people does have some meaning. However, there is a world of difference in how you are seen by a prospective employer if you can specify where in personnel/human resources you wish to be. Look at the difference between these two objectives:

Objective A: A position in personnel
Objective B: A position in training and development.

Objective B is much more precise and shows you have done your homework. It also limits your further research. You do not have to learn about compensation systems or other activities unconnected to your interests.

Within every industry there are expanding human resource needs. The insurance and banking industries, as two examples, are faced with major employee problems. The rapid turnover of people in these two industries points to the need for better recruitment and training.

A good job hunting principle is to be aware of legislation which causes changes in today's organizations. If you are interested in Human Resources, focus on laws which affect this function. The status of specific companies regarding Equal Employment Opportunity (EEO) legislation is illustrative. Even if companies have complied with federal regulations concerning the hiring of minorities, needs still exist in the area of educating employees regarding their career development possibilities.

Occupational Safety and Health Administration (OSHA) legislation is another force affecting this function. New health programs are being encouraged—executive physical fitness; substance abuse programs for employees with drug or alcohol problems; employee counseling programs for general emotional health, etc.

Communications

Communications (also frequently known as Public Relations, Public Affairs, or External Relations) is another rapidly developing function. Growth here is a result of changes in society which have created increasing needs for better relations between organizations and the publics with whom they deal. A good communications function today is responding to and bringing about positive social change. Contrast with this the previous practice of merely image building in times of crisis.

This function is structured around the different publics who are of concern to companies. The following activities are commonly found under this function.

Customer Relations Building and maintaining positive relations with consumers and consumer groups.

Government Relations Monitoring and affecting legislation that impacts the company at federal, state, and local levels.

Investor Relations Informing professional investors regarding the company's prospects.

Media Relations Nurturing positive relations with press and broadcast personnel. Preparing press kits, "backgrounders," press releases.

Community Relations Maintaining positive relations with the local community.

International Relations Executing the full range of corporate communications in foreign countries.

Creative Services Preparing photography, graphics, and written materials for use in the promotional literature of the company.

Employee Communications Informing employees of company policy and programs through in-house newspapers, etc.

In approaching this function in specific organizations, you should be certain that the activity being approached is actually located under this function. It is a common practice to locate relations with different publics under other functions. Frequently relations with the financial public is placed under the Finance function. Similarly, communicating with employees as a public is often placed under Human Resource Development. You will notice it is missing from Figure 16. Customer relations units are sometimes placed under the Marketing function, etc. When you approach a specific organization, know in advance where the activity

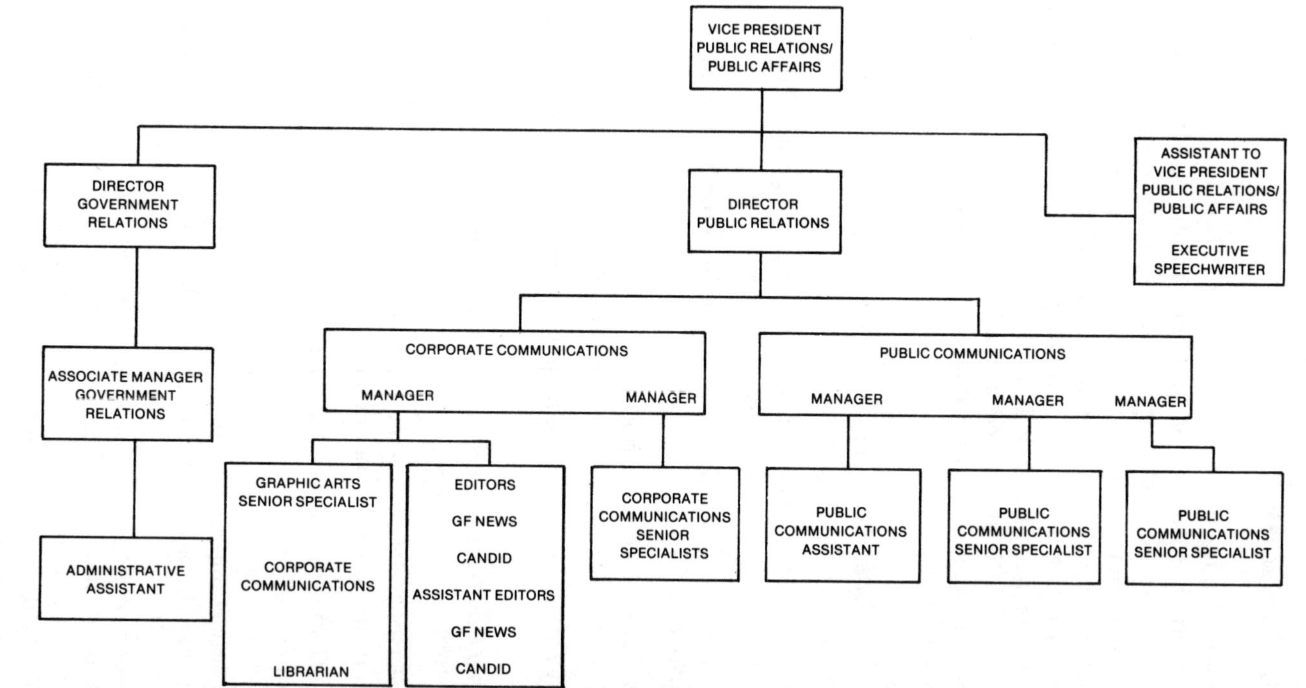

FIGURE 16 The Communication Function of General Foods Corporation, Combining Public Relations, Public Affairs, and Government Relations. From Report 679, *Managing Corporate External Relations* (New York: The Conference Board, 1976), p. 31, by permission of The Conference Board.

you are targeting is placed. This will enable you to identify the appropriate people to contact, as well as give you some understanding of how the organization views this activity.

If you are interested in the Communications function, you should obviously be skilled in communicating. Writing and speaking skills are extremely important. Research abilities are also crucial. If you are to communicate effectively to a specific public you must know what that public is thinking and feeling. Therefore gathering information is fundamental.

If you have creative, artistic skills, you may also be interested in this function since brochures, films, and media are important means of communication. Request copies of annual reports from several companies and look over these handsome productions. A corporate communications staff was probably responsible for putting the reports together.

Marketing

The purpose of marketing is to promote, distribute, and sell the organization's products or services at the highest level of profitability. Historically this function was synonymous with sales. Effectiveness was measured by sheer volume of sales, and percentage or share of the market secured. The changes occurring today involve activities concerned with more sophisticated planning and control. Due to the increased costs of production, lower levels of productivity, and increased cost of storage and distribution, sheer volume of sales is no longer an adequate measure of real performance. New concepts of product/line profitability are beginning to dominate market planning activities.

The following activities are found in the marketing function:

Market Research Monitoring market trends, competition, the company's profitability; conducting media and advertising research, and compiling all information relevant to various markets and promotional activities.

Sales Research Setting quotas for salesmen, forecasting sales, controlling and monitoring inventories and distribution costs, designing sales inventories, and conducting sales analyses.

Product Research and Development Testing new products and ideas, analyzing product image and features, developing and test marketing new products, monitoring competitive products.

Product/Sales Management Actively coordinating promotion, distribution, and sales of the company's product.

Advertising and Promotion Creating promotional materials and campaigns, writing copy, creating graphics and art work, packaging the product, and general merchandising.

Figure 17 gives a table of organization for the marketing function.

It becomes obvious from looking at these various activities that the marketing function comprises much more than sales. As mentioned before, the changes in this function are with the research, planning, and control activities. There is little people contact in many of the planning and research activities. In fact, facility with statistics and numbers would be of prime importance. If you want to enter the sales field and feel that your skills lie in this area, it is important to believe in what you sell. The days of the used car salesman bending an elbow with the customers, or Willy Loman slowly dying on his treadmill because of lack of belief are going fast. Tomorrow's effective sales person will be one who believes in his product and knows it thoroughly.

Finance

The activities of the Finance function fall into several broad areas.

Obtaining Financing Selling stock; securing long-term loans from outside sources such as banks, insurance companies, or security underwriters; and securing short-term loans.

Safeguarding Company Funds (cash on hand and/or on deposit in banks, or in short-term securities). This includes:

> *Cash Management* Forecasting cash flow, establishing systems and procedures for handling cash.
>
> *Credit and Collections* Granting credit to customers to stimulate sales and collecting due accounts.
>
> *Administering Insurance Policies and Pension Funds* to increase their value.

Managing Financial Information, Accounting Analyzing and preparing all financial statements; compiling and controlling all financial documents such as bills, sales invoices, etc.

Long-range Planning and Budgeting Administering long-range economic forecasting and appraisal, capital expenditure and income budgeting; establishing cost standards; and internal auditing.

Tax Management Paying all corporate taxes as well as collecting and disbursing customer and employee taxes.

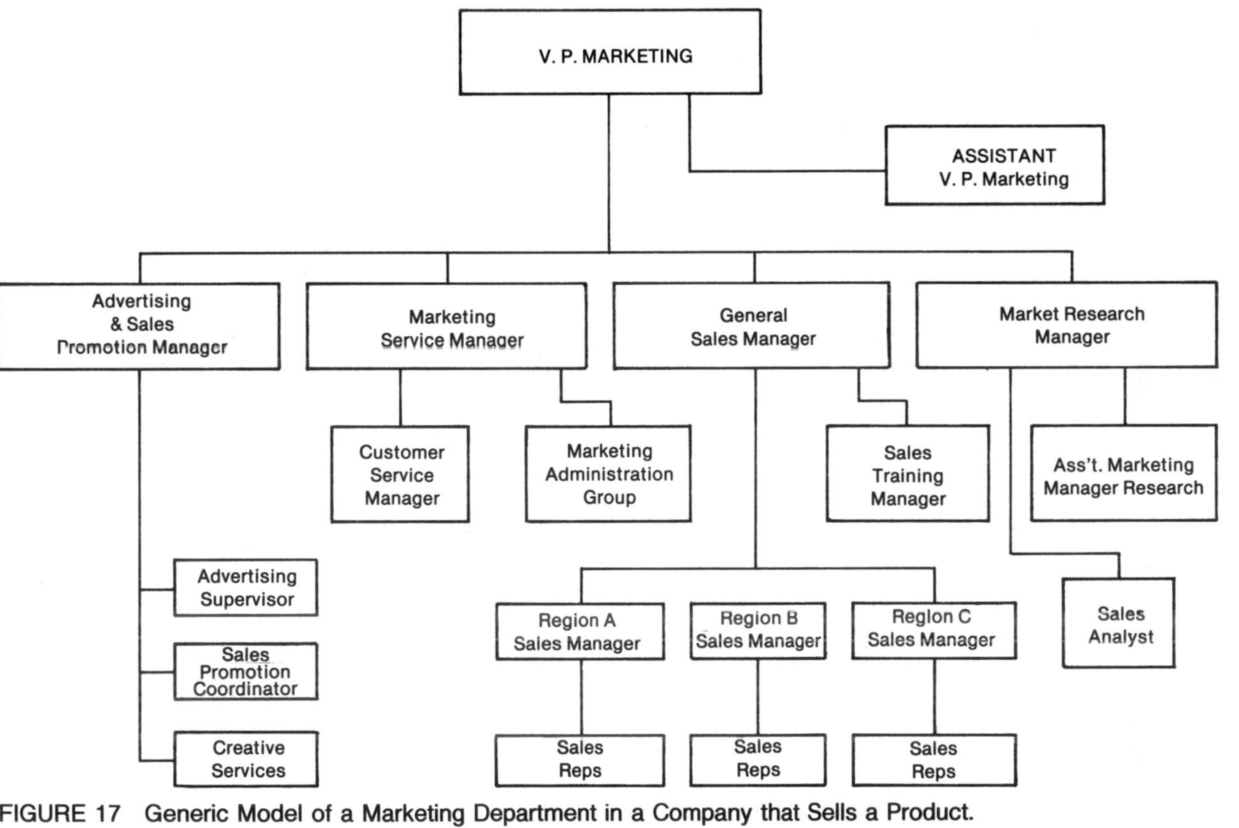

FIGURE 17 Generic Model of a Marketing Department in a Company that Sells a Product.

Mergers and Acquisitions Analyzing and executing the purchase of other companies, defending the company against unwelcome takeovers, and negotiating advantageous mergers or joint ventures.

Figure 18 shows the structure of the Finance function. Notice that data processing, what is called in the model Information Services, is located in this chart within the Finance function. In most large companies, data processing methods started in the finance department. Nowadays they pervade the entire organization.

The Finance function as a whole tends to deal heavily with figures. Accounting deals with figures in a very concrete way, while financial planning demands the same facility with figures but deals with them in a more abstract fashion. Frequently job searchers equate this function with bookkeeping and accounting. If they did not enjoy long lists of addition and subtraction in school, they give no further thought to careers in this function. By looking at the definitions of the activities, you will see that many more skills are involved than simply mathematics.

Research and Development

American companies have always been known for their attention to research. Technological breakthroughs in electronics and new materials enabled Neil Armstrong to be the first man on the moon. Similar research genius has put American companies in the forefront of many industries, computer technology, for example.

Research and development remains central to organizational innovation and there are signs today that large American companies are in need of renewed energies in this function. The difficulty of fostering the creative spirit in large, sometimes cumbersome organizations, is a recognized phenomenon. It is difficult for anyone to be truly creative if the results of the creativity do not in some way belong to the creator. The R&D function suffers currently from this problem; the large corporations generally are lagging in productivity as a result of people feeling unrelated to their work. The return of a vital, creative spirit to the R&D function will depend upon management innovations that restore some form of ownership of work to employees.

The R&D function employs technically trained individuals. Depending on the industry, various technical competencies and training are needed. Backgrounds in engineering, chemistry, physiology, biology,

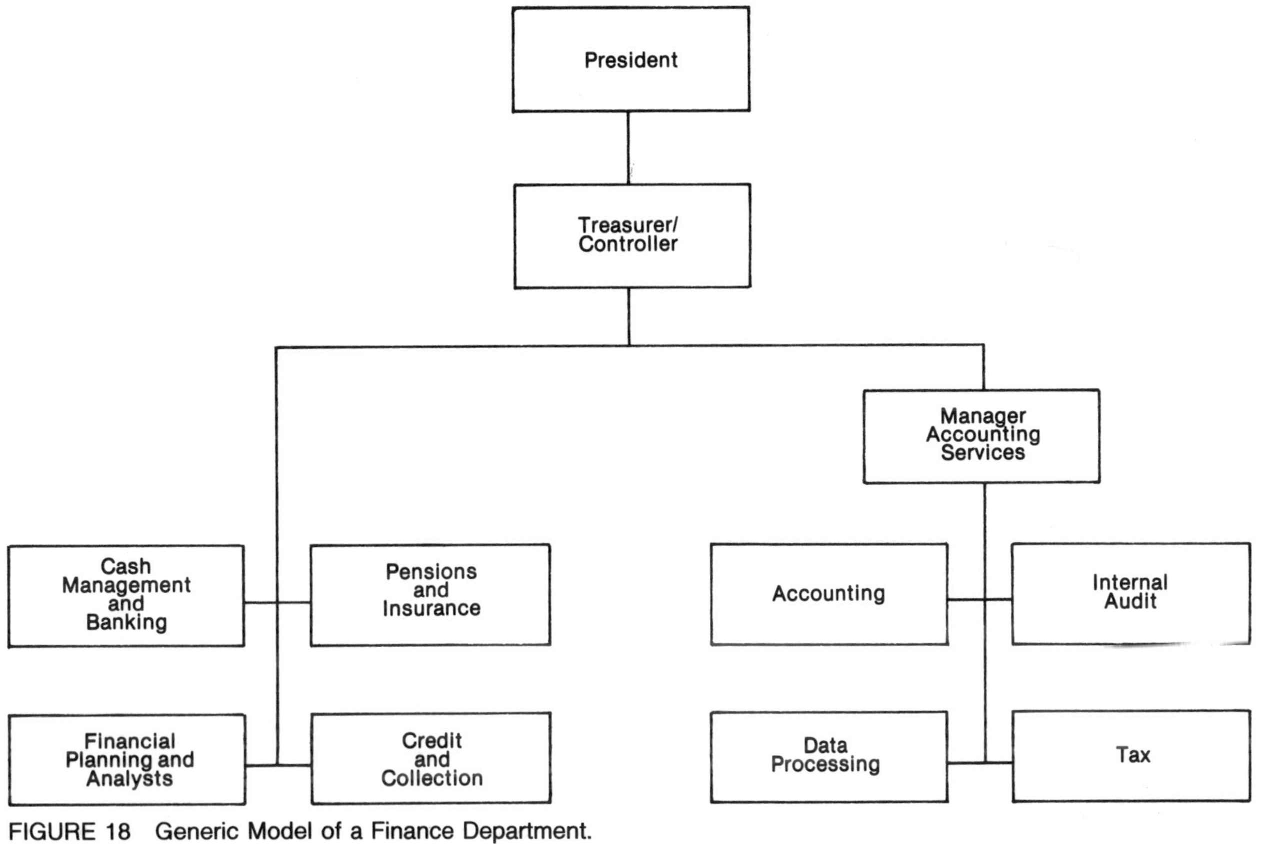

FIGURE 18 Generic Model of a Finance Department.

physics, psychology, ecology, and sociology appear frequently in the R&D field.

The activities within this function include:

Pure Research Developing new concepts that can be converted into new products or services.

Product Quality Control Improving the quality of existing products, and maintaining quality standards during the production process.

Product Engineering Designing new methodologies and production procedures.

New Product Development Converting pure research and new procedures into new products, as well as adapting existing products to new markets.

Operations/Administration

Operations is the function which defines the activities most central to the nature of the organization. Industries are also defined by this function. The Standard Industrial Classification (SIC) Manual, a standard reference, is an index which groups industries according to numerical classifications attached to products and services. It has eighty-nine broad categories from agricultural crop production to miscellaneous services. Under each broad category there are as many as fifty subheadings. Familiarity with this index will provide you with one overview of the world of work classified by industry products and/or services.

Since the operations function defines the industry, the industry also influences how this function is carried out. Organizations which produce a product will differ somewhat in their operations function from organizations which provide a service. Recognizing that these differences will exist, the activities under operations within the model are:

Manufacturing/Extraction Producing the product or service.

Shipping Overseeing delivery of products or services to centers of use or distribution.

Purchasing Obtaining materials for the production of products or services.

Maintenance Ensuring that equipment for producing the product is maintained, or that services are adequately delivered.

Security Protecting facilities and materials.

Travel Organizing travel arrangements for company personnel.

Contract Administration Assuring that contracts with suppliers or customers are fulfilled.

Figure 19 is a chart of the Operations function of an airline, which is an industry providing a service. Note that the marketing and personnel functions are included under Operations in this instance.

If you as a job seeker have an industry preference, you are probably interested in some activity within Operations. For example, if you say you are interested in the book publishing industry, assuming you know little about the industry, you are probably interested in editing books. Editing is an activity within Operations for book publishing. Interestingly, seven out of ten applicants to book publishing are seeking editorial positions.

FUNCTIONS—AN OVERVIEW

The following is a summary and overview of the functions that constitute the organizational expression of work.

Personnel/Human Resources

Recruitment
Compensation
Labor Relations
Benefits
Safety and Health
Equal Employment Opportunity
(Employee Communications)
Organization Development
Training and Development
Manpower Planning

Communications

Customer Relations
Government Relations
Investor Relations
Media Relations
Community Relations
International Relations
Creative Services
(Employee Communications)

Marketing

Market Research
Sales Research
(Product Research and Development)
Product/Sales Management
Advertising and Promotion

Finance

Cash Management
Credit and Collections
Pensions and Insurance
Accounting
Long-Range Planning
Budgeting
Tax Management
Mergers and Acquisitions

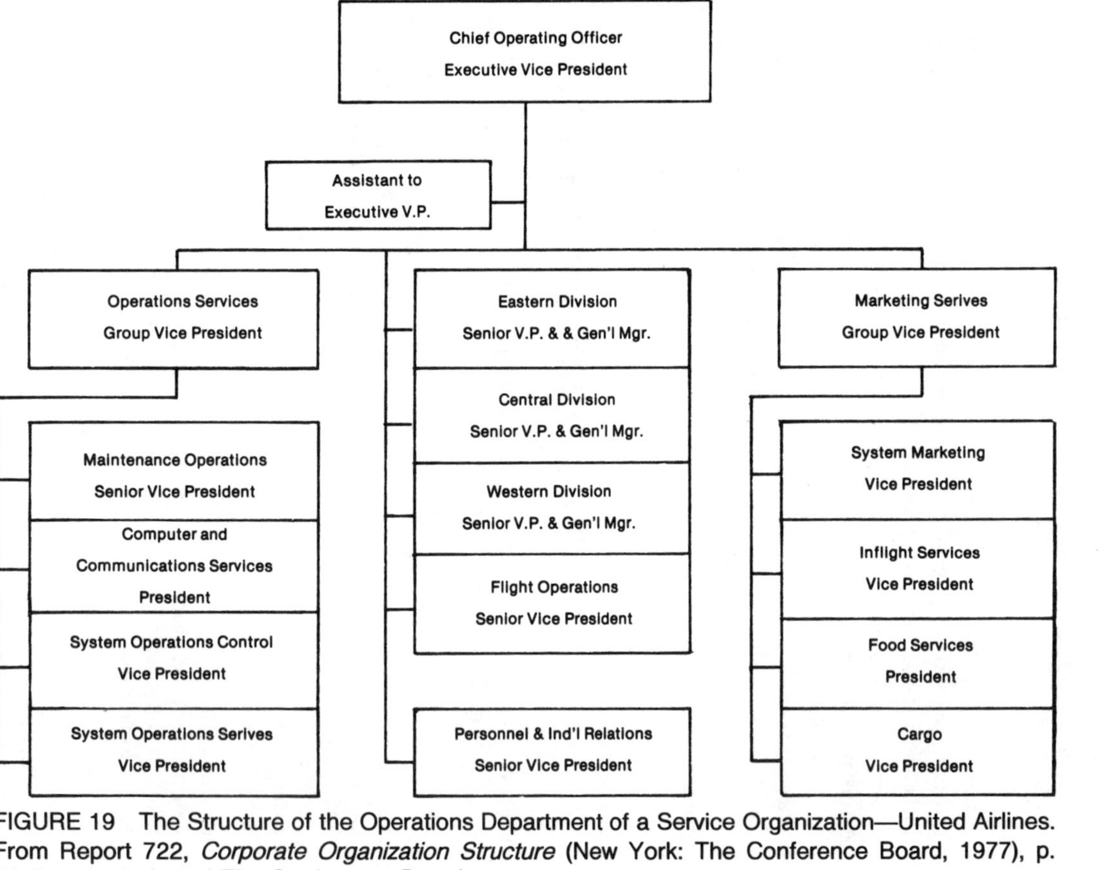

FIGURE 19 The Structure of the Operations Department of a Service Organization—United Airlines. From Report 722, *Corporate Organization Structure* (New York: The Conference Board, 1977), p. 54, by permission of The Conference Board.

Research and Development

Pure Research
Product Quality Control
Product Engineering
(New Product Development)

Operations/Administration

Manufacturing/Extraction
Shipping
Purchasing
Maintenance
Security
Travel
Contract Administration

We have put parentheses around three activities since their position often varies across organizations. Today, New Product Development is split between Marketing and R & D; Employee Communications is split between Personnel and Communications; Internal Auditing is split between Finance and the Legal Department.

THE CROSS-FUNCTIONAL SERVICE AREAS

In addition to the six functions, two very important cross-functional services make up our model. Let us look briefly at each.

Information Systems

The development in recent years of sophisticated information processing equipment such as computers and high speed copying equipment has begun to revolutionize modern organizations. With the initial clouds of confusion and suspicion ending, information systems are being developed for use in all functions. As noted before, the Finance function was the first to employ the new technologies for accounting, payroll, and billing purposes. The applications today in marketing, operations, human resources, and research and development are growing rapidly.

In the future, employment opportunities within this service will be found in every function. If you have career goals in any function, you should become familiar with the new technologies which are being used within that function. Marketing information systems, for example, is an activity that provides many new opportunities. Information systems in Human Resources are a definite part of the future and create new opportunities, as that function gathers more and more data for planning purposes.

Legal Services

The legal services in modern organizations also cross all functions. With the growth of new legislation and government regulatory agencies, each function needs specialized legal advice. The following list provides a sample of legislative and regulatory concerns that impact different functions. It is a brief sampling, since there are hundreds of laws and agencies affecting modern organizations.

Personnel/Human Resources Departments of Labor; Health, Education, and Welfare; laws such as safety and health (OSHA); equal employment opportunity (EEO).

Communications Government bodies in general are monitored within this function.

Marketing Department of Justice; price fixing and anti-trust legislation.

Finance Department of Labor; Security and Exchange Commission (SEC); pension (ERISA); and financial disclosure legislation.

R&D Department of Justice; Environmental Protection Agency (EPA); laws dealing with patents and copyrights; toxic substance legislation (for specific industries).

Operations/Administration deals with government agencies which are industry related, e.g., Food and Drug Administration (FDA) for food and drug manufacturers; the Federal Reserve Board for banks, etc.

Figure 20 is a chart of E. F. Hutton's Legal & Compliance Department.

Job searchers should be aware that legal departments employ more than attorneys. For people with auditing skills or interests in surveillance, you may find positions in legal/compliance departments similar to E. F. Hutton's. The way into such a department would be as a junior auditor or surveillance analyst. With interest in these activities, a liberal arts background is sufficient.

MANAGEMENT

Management is a service which takes place in all functions within organizations as a means of coordinating activities so that purposes are accomplished. The service areas also require management.

With the rapid expansion of organizations after World War II,

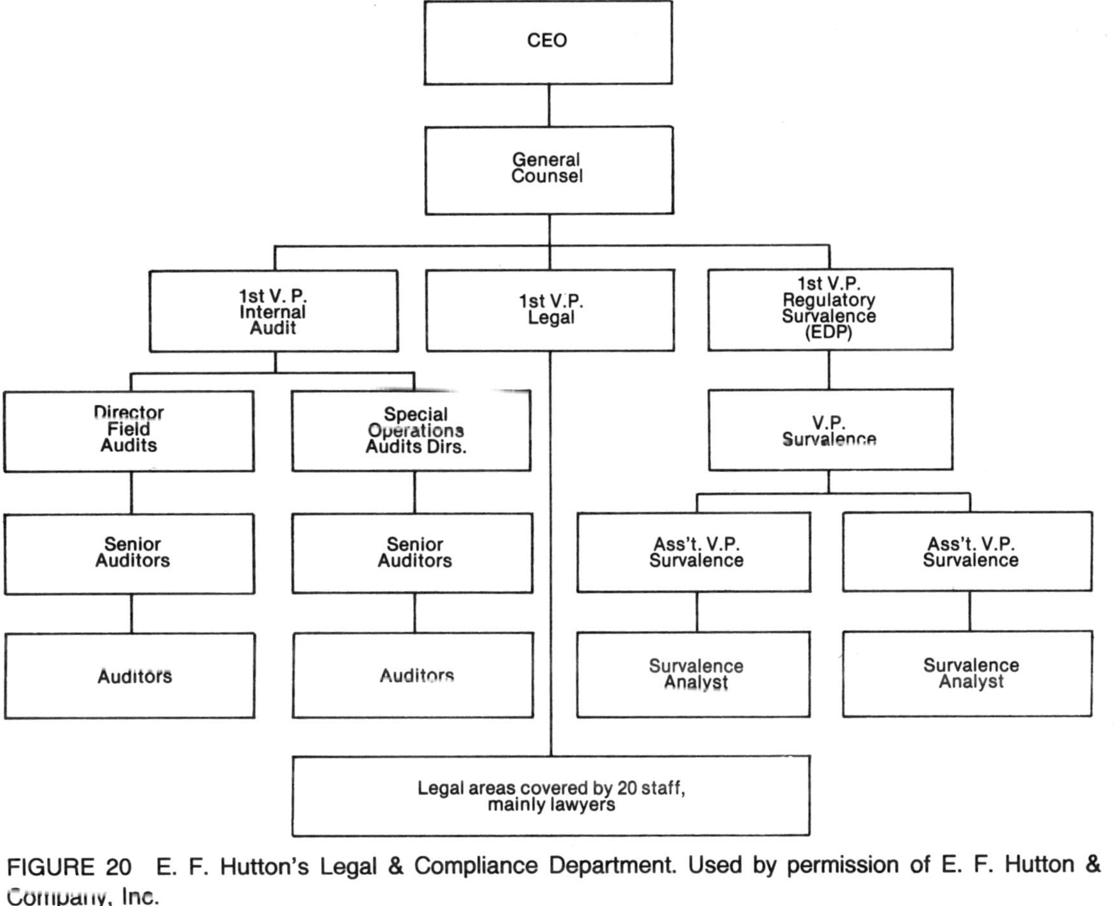

FIGURE 20 E. F. Hutton's Legal & Compliance Department. Used by permission of E. F. Hutton & Company, Inc.

management needs increased significantly. From first line supervisors and ever increasing numbers of middle managers, to upper level vice-presidents, the ranks grew. Today with increased needs to control costs, middle level positions are not growing as rapidly as before. In fact there are signs of retrenchment at this level.

Management has today become a science as well as an art. Graduate Business Administration (MBA) programs have increased four-fold in the last five years, a sure sign of the need for better trained personnel to manage today's organizations.

There are many definitions of management, yet most people agree that good management includes abilities in planning, organizing, decision-making, motivating, and evaluating. In the past, people were put into management positions because of purely technical knowledge or ability. They often had little skill in dealing with people. In the future, managers will need more sophisticated skills in communication and motivation as well as technical abilities.

SUMMARY

Once you become familiar with the variety of activities which are performed in organizational functions, you will be able to link your interests and skills to specific work activities. Linking interests and skills to the nature of work helps you in a way that pure self-analysis cannot. When you understand the nature of work, you can overcome a major obstacle in choosing your career: lack of information on where your skills and interests fit.

In every function there are changes occurring which can be related to the perspective on development presented in Chapter 2. These trends create job opportunities you can take advantage of once you understand how to meet the needs created by these changes. In the next chapter these changes will be presented in some detail as an aid to help you link your style compass to the organization model.

ORGANIZATIONAL NEEDS AND CAREER DEVELOPMENT

PURPOSE

The circle containing the four styles of functioning gave you a method for considering the whole of yourself. The organizational model provides a method for considering the whole of an organization and how work is expressed through its functional components. In this chapter, we want to use these circles to help you develop personal career plans that relate to the major needs of organizations in the coming decade. The needs presented here will give you material to begin thinking of specific areas in which to approach potential employers. The development of organizations in the 1980s will take place in relation to these needs.

At the present moment business organizations in this country are at a turning point. The laws on which they have operated so far must change as they move into a new phase of development. Like the crisis at the middle of life which each of us faces, organizations now stand face to face with their neglected, undeveloped side in a mid-life crossroads of their own. Their future depends on whether their leaders understand the transition they are experiencing. As we have said repeatedly this understanding derives from having gone through such changes in personal life, from knowing firsthand how the world works and being able, as well as willing, to use this knowledge to improve things. Organizations are in trouble in our society mostly because so few people truly enjoy working for them. Disinterest and depression are behind the lack of productivity. Until we solve these issues, efforts at curing the problem are mere band aids. What is needed is the collaboration of everyone within organizations to begin working toward new ways of operating. This is the long march necessary to improve the quality of our working lives. In discussing organizations in this chapter, the focus will be on corporations involved in commerce. Their size and central role in development make them important influences when it comes to the working life of most people.

Following World War II, corporations in this country began an expansion program unparalleled in history. Now this kind of growth is over and the world economy has radically changed, with energy being an uncertain resource. The way organizational leaders have been taught to think, to plan and to act now deserves serious scrutiny and challenge. Growth in size can no longer be the basic goal in long range planning, yet it remains so in most corporations. What must be recognized is that the growth of the past was at the expense of human realities and ecological necessities that are now demanding attention. This is the heart of the challenge of the next decade and should be at the center of your career planning. Seeing your own part in the struggle to change the fundamentals on which organizations have been operating is a major step toward restoring meaning in work. No matter where you are in an organization or what it is you're doing, you can be part of the effort to create a new spirit. In order to understand what will be involved in this transition, let's examine some of the basic premises on which corporations have operated in the past.

THE OLD LAW OF CORPORATE DEVELOPMENT

In their growth up to the present, the major corporations of the world have operated on a set of principles that together make up a kind of law. This law was the basis of their development so far, and, like the law of the first half of life for an individual, it too must change as the second half begins. A turning point has been reached making the old law obsolete. Let's examine the principles on which this old law rests and consider how they must change.

Profit

The first principle has to do with how profit is considered in a business operation.

> The basic purpose of any business is to make a profit. The greater the profit, the better—profit should be unrestricted.

No business can survive if part of this principle is not honored. Yet we now face a worldwide situation where unrestricted profit as an operating principle threatens the stability of the globe. As soon as there is any hint of restricting profit or modifying it in relation to the needs of the whole, the business community often stiffens and cries "socialism!" This reaction makes discussion difficult and frequently so emotional that the important facts and issues cannot be examined. Despite the difficulty, every corporation in the world has got to begin asking questions about its profits in relation to responsibility for the whole. Commerce governs the relationship between nations and is the major force for stability. The leaders within commerce have the opportunity now to take the responsibility that goes with their power. Some have begun to do so as they involve themselves in important issues of corporate social responsibility. But in other cases, there still appears to be a myopia that is dangerous for the eighties.

Concern for the whole in regard to this first principle relates to the nation first of all and then to the total community of nations. There are significant recent examples of disregard for both. Take the home heating oil and jet fuel controversy in the United States. Because the market price for jet fuel was higher than that of heating oil, companies were diverting their heating oil allocations to the jet fuel market, in one case threatening the supply of the entire state of New Hampshire. Only government intervention stopped an entire state from being deprived of its heating oil. But clearly, the federal government should not serve as a constant policeman. Only an internal leadership capable of seeing beyond the need for bigger and bigger profits can rectify this kind of problem. The worldwide problem of the transnational corporations exploiting the less developed countries is a central issue for the total community of nations. The growing polarization between rich and poor nations can only be alleviated if the leaders in the transnational corporations become sensitive to this split and deal with the profit factor accordingly. Because commerce governs the modern world and is its major stabilizing force, the leaders within its ranks are capable of healing the fractured world community in a way no other organizational setting can. This is the real challenge of the eighties to the business community and offers innumerable career opportunities for those concerned with the world as a whole.

Relationship of Function and Person

A second principle has to do with the relationship of function and person in the management of organizations.

> Function is primary. Person is subservient to function for the sake of efficient management.

Management theory from its inception has been wrestling with this tension between function or task to be performed and the person involved. Initially in management theory the stress was on function, then there was considerable reaction to the absence of concern for the human factor. But the debate goes on as various management styles are discussed in contemporary journals. In all the discussion there still appears too much of an either–or resolution, and too few genuinely new *images* that bring the person and function together in authentic ways. If management views its work force as persons, many things would develop within modern organizations to improve their quality. Here and there new images are emerging where management and labor collaborate in truly personal fashion, and functions are performed in a highly efficient manner. The Work in America Institute in Scarsdale, New York (700 White Plains Road, 10583), founded to advance productivity and the quality of working life, has been gathering data on corporate success stories related to new images of management—labor collaboration. At a national conference in 1980, the Institute presented six of these stories. They are summarized briefly here.*

> *Dana Corporation.* This leading manufacturer of components for the transportation industry realized that one of the best techniques for improving productivity was to share the gains with the workers who were responsible for increased efficiency and profitability. With this in mind, Dana instituted a method based on the Scanlon Plan whereby the union and management became actively involved in improving both productivity and quality of working life. As a result, everyone benefited: the customer . . . plant . . . employee . . .

* Used by permission of the Work in America Institute.

and community. Among the achievements: costs have been reduced every year in the range of 10 to 20 percent.

Towne Robinson Fastener. The team approach to problem solving is at the heart of the Towne Robinson Fastener Company's productivity improvement program. This Dearborn, Michigan subsidiary of Key International, Inc. is a supplier of metal parts to the automotive industry. Consultant Sidney Rubenstein began working with management and union leaders who, in turn, worked to train their representatives. Soon supervisors and hourly workers were involved in team building and problem solving. The results: improved quality of working life and increased productivity.

Rockwell International. One of the most expensive, complex, and hardest used pieces of machinery in the world is the web offset press. And Rockwell's graphic systems division is the largest supplier of these presses in the world. In this exacting business, the problems of quality control and productivity are crucial. Rockwell International in Pittsburgh, PA maintains their extraordinarily high standards by involving management and workers. Quality control circles, so successful in Japan, are adapted to the needs of this situation. The circles invite the worker into the decision making process in a significant way.

Midland-Ross. At this Tennessee plant which manufactures rough wiring equipment for the building industry, both quality and quantity of production have been markedly improved. In addition, grievances, absenteeism, and employee turnover have been substantially reduced. The secret: a Scanlon Plan which makes workers partners in the gains of increased productivity.

American Telephone and Telegraph. How do you introduce new technology in diverse organizations scattered throughout the vast Bell System without disruptive side effects? AT&T devised a unique human performance committee system which deals in new work methods, design of work, skill retraining, and career planning for displaced personnel. The committee allows for participation of employees in establishing performance standards. The results: new systems and technologies achieve their performance objectives with reasonable ease and efficiency.

Lincoln National Life. How do you increase productivity—not only within a small department or organization—but on a huge scale? Lincoln National recognized the need to train several thousand managers and their employees to become more responsible and

> responsive. A top management team was behind this effort. The educational process, employee attitudes toward the change process, and the results to date all indicate significant progress.

These are promising new images that go beyond the worn out either–or debates about person and function and point the way toward major organization development efforts for the eighties. Within these stories are significant trends to which you can relate your career planning efforts. The Scanlon Plan mentioned in these descriptions involves collaborative planning between labor and management on productivity goals and profit sharing. Developed by the late Joseph P. Scanlon, a former union official, the plan is based on the concept that the employee, the employer, and the union have much in common. It relates directly to the concern for the whole now required in the development of organizations. It is significant that the former head of the Dana Corporation has recently become the Dean of Stanford University's business school, one of the most prestigious producers of business leaders in the country.

Environment

Principle three relates to environment.

> Environment is not a systematic consideration in the day-to-day operation of business, except what is forced on an organization by government or political pressures.

Examples of the destruction of land and waters by corporations within various industries are by now well known. Still there is an insufficient sense of the unity of man as a species and all that surrounds him. Environment is still not considered important in most business decisions, and only regulation backed by legal penalty prevents continued and more widespread destruction. The energy crisis will demand that environment become a central and sacred reality in all organizational decisions. Environment will be seen not just as something to avoid polluting, but as something to be developed and cared for in specific ways. Conservation will become a major part of business planning.

Growth

Because of the growing importance of conservation a fourth principle concerning growth will have to change.

> Planning is based on continued growth as a systematic projection.

Long-range planning is based on these growth assumptions. This will be one of the most difficult principles to change as it is so basic to business life to date. To even think of zero growth as a planning assumption is like death. However, the life of an organization in the next decade may depend upon how creatively it can plan in new ways not dependent on growth in size. The fact that less can be more will be accepted as a principle on the personal level for a growing number of people may make it easier for business leaders. More will be said about this later on in this chapter. The quality of organizational life can then be attended to as well as the quality of product and service.

Ownership and Profits

A final principle has to do with ownership of the large corporations.

> Ownership and profits belong to a minority most often unrelated to the labor force.

In the epigraph to this book, two voices from opposite sides of the world's political spectrum point to the danger of separating work and ownership. When a Pope John Paul II and a Fidel Castro can agree strongly on an issue, it is obviously of central significance to the world. It is certainly central to organizational development for the world's corporations. Participative ownership through profit sharing, stock options, and other ways of acquiring a stake in the business have already begun. Chief executive officers with vision, like James F. Bere of Borg-Warner Corporation, are calling for a second industrial revolution which puts people at the center of things and includes participative ownership * Bere also calls for a new kind of cost accounting that treats people as the prime asset of business, a steady job and assured annual wage for every employee, participative management, and even regular sabbaticals where people can try out long-held dreams and get "repotted." Leaders like this are the hope of the eighties and provide direction for meaningful career plans.

As a way of summarizing the changes needed in these five principles underlying the law of corporate development so far, look at Figure 21. Corporate life is at a turning point where the old law (left column) on which it operated must change to a new law (right column). Career

* James F. Bere, *Management Review* (July, 1978), pp. 18–22.

Old Law	New Law
Principles:	Principles:
Profit should be unrestricted.	Profit should be conditioned by the needs of the whole.
Person is subservient to function.	Function follows person.
Environment is not a systematic consideration.	The corporation must be ecologically responsible.
Planning is based on projections of continued growth.	Conservation and zero growth are planning assumptions. Less can be more.
Ownership and profits are unrelated to labor.	Participative ownership is esential to productivity.

FIGURE 21 Shift in Principles of Corporate Development.

planning for the eighties should consider these new principles as creating the *direction* for organization development.

Moving from the old to the new law will, of course, not be easy. It will necessitate a lot of struggle and some painful changes. Seeing your part in this struggle adds a dimension to career and personal work that provides a connection to the whole which is necessary to meaning. This shift of new principles will have impact on each of the organizational functions described in Chapter 3. You can relate your career planning to the specific changes that will occur in these functions and think about these changes in relation to the development of the whole. The next section will assist you in this effort.

ORGANIZATIONAL FUNCTIONS: HOW WILL THEY CHANGE?

Each of the organizational functions described in Chapter 3 is changing in specific ways. Your career planning should consider these changes as they affect your objectives. It is often possible to create opportunities, if you have carefully thought out ways of dealing with the needs of a particular function. Let's consider each function in turn to see how it is changing and what needs are surfacing in each.

Human Resource Development is a function which has been changing rapidly, as you saw in Chapter 3. What was once considered a minor function in most organizations has now taken on significance due to regulations monitoring personnel practices, as well as the changing nature of the work force itself. These two influences will continue to shape this function during the coming decade. Job planning and second career opportunities for growing numbers of people will be big developments as more and more personal control over work will be demanded. Personnel surveys promise to become important sources of communication and aids to planning. The largest companies already have permanent and specialized staff for this task—smaller companies will move in a similar direction. Planning itself will become more scientific, and be based on data gathered carefully and stored in information retrieval systems that will play a central role in the function. Beneath all these trends will be the shift in principles described earlier as organizations struggle to restore the human dimension that has been lost.

Education and training are on the increase within large organizations as they strive to keep up with incessant change. It is increasingly impossible to prepare people in school settings for what they face on the job. So you can expect industry to establish more job-related education and training. This education will be based on the best methodologies available with all appropriate audio-visual and technological back-up being employed. Evaluation of these efforts will be a central concern as business insists on efficiency and cost effectiveness. You may well see the universities looking to the educational programs in industry to learn something about being more efficient and effective themselves. Corporations do not suffer from the prejudices that fragment university faculties and prevent quality education from being produced on campus. They are free to take the best that's available and use it to educate people for their organizational responsibilities. In this area, human resource development promises to offer real opportunity during the eighties.

Communications is a function being deeply affected by the growing interdependence of the world community. No organization hoping to act effectively can afford to ignore this interdependence. Clear statements of each organization's objectives will be given to the public as well as to its employees. In the past such communication might have been seen as a way of shading the truth, to always keep the company in a favorable light. Today the public is sophisticated enough not to be fooled by such shadings, and the interconnectedness of the globe almost compels honest communication. The sooner organizations move fully toward this honesty, both toward their employees and their publics, the sooner they will be able to establish the balance needed in this important function. Media relations will change as investigative reporting intensifies and executives learn how to deal directly with a concerned public. Employee communications will develop beyond mere house newspapers talking about the latest outing to serious discussions of policy and objectives in a variety of forums. This is one of the fastest growing specialties of corporate communications. Government relations will also change as more of a collaboration develops and the present adversary tone diminishes. Customer relations will concentrate on quality service and quality products backed up by quick responses to complaints. In each of these trends are opportunities for career planning.

Marketing and its related activities will rely more and more on data-gathering techniques as various marketing information systems are incorporated into the function. Meeting needs instead of trying to create and manipulate them will become the name of the game. The hard sell, the exaggerated image are already bankrupt marketing practices even though they still abound. Finding effective ways of telling the truth about a product or service will make for effective and successful marketing practice in the 1980s. A number of organizations that have never had to compete in the marketplace may begin adding the marketing function, making for a lot of opportunity. This happened recently with American Telephone and Telegraph and may well increase as disenchantment with big government's regulation grows and competition in the marketplace takes over as the regulatory principle.

Research and Development will intensify as the energy sources that organizations have traditionally depended upon continue to change. Appropriate or alternative technologies have become centrally important because of the energy situation. These new technologies will be the focus of R&D activity during the eighties in every industry. Imagination to design these new approaches and the technical skills to carry them out will be in high demand within this function. R&D expenditures will increase and opportunities expand for those who have the requisite background and ability.

Finance as a function was characterized in the seventies by tightened and increased controls. Often those who headed this function were made chief executive officers because of their knowledge of careful accounting and control procedures. As we move into an age of conservation and scarcity these controls will grow in importance. Redundancy planning is being talked about more and more as management realizes the need for even more controls and scaling down. Look for the finance function to become more conservative as well as imaginative during the next decade—a time of profound transition for all organizations.

Operations will be strongly influenced by the energy crisis and shifting management values. Long-range planning techniques that consider the important new principles are already being connected to operational decisions. This activity will grow and environmental issues will become most important. Regional activity will be likely to increase as the energy crunch makes national scope less practical. There are enormous opportunities in this return to regional development. Cottage industries, once passé, will see a resurgence as large companies begin returning operations to regional and local control.

In all of the functions that have been described, development has been one-sided. If this same kind of emphasis continues, each function will fail to meet the real demands of the present as it becomes progressively obsolete. Gregory Bateson defines obsolescence as a function of such one-sided progress in his book, *Mind and Nature.* He draws parallels between mental processes and the biological processes of evolution, showing how crucial it is to maintain the balance of the whole of any system if it is to survive. Similarly, the survival of organizations as we know them depends upon their avoiding the obsolescence of one-sidedness. Bateson also examines university education, calling it a rip-off because of its current obsolescence. There is a war going on in the university community between what he calls rigor and imagination—another way of describing what has been labeled here the Structural and Oceanic tendencies. The issue is summarized succinctly by Bateson: "Rigor alone is paralytic death, but imagination alone is insanity."* It requires wisdom to bring the two together—the statesmanship of the true leader. Such leadership has never been more necessary within every organization that makes up contemporary society. Because this issue is so central to the coming decade, it must likewise be central to your career planning. If you think about your own work as it relates to these major conflicts within organizations, you will be able to contribute significantly to their resolution. You also have the opportunity to create the sense of meaning that has been lost in most work since the Industrial Revolution. By restoring the connection of personal work to the whole of your life, it is possible to bring back its dignity and meaning. Wherever we work these days, we work for the survival of the planet and all its natural systems. If we fail to do this, we contribute to the destruction, pollution and one-sidedness that leads to obsolescence.

SOME LESSONS FROM THE PAST

There are some valuable lessons from the recent past on pitfalls to avoid in working with organizations experiencing change. If you consider the sixties, the organizational settings that experienced the most signifi-

* Gregory Bateson, *Mind and Nature* (New York: E. P. Dutton, 1979), p. 219.

cant upheaval were the churches and the schools, especially the universities.

One thing we have learned from the sixties is that the youth culture and its revolt was terribly one-sided. To return to Bateson for a moment, he puts it well in his memorandum to the Regents of the University of California.

> Tweedledum and Tweedledee *agreed* to have a battle; and isn't it a blessing that the contrasting generations can agree that social "power" has physical dimensions and can engage in battles for this strange abstraction. (In other times and other places, battles were fought for "honor," "beauty," and even "truth" . . .)
>
> Looking at the whole mess from another angle, I believe that the students were right in the sixties: There was something very wrong in their education and indeed in almost the whole culture. But I believe that they were wrong in their diagnosis of where the trouble lay. They fought for "representation" and "power." On the whole, they won their battles and now we have student representation on the Board of Regents and elsewhere. But it becomes increasingly clear that the winning of these battles for "power" has made no difference in the educational process. The obsolescence to which I referred is unchanged and, no doubt, in a few years we shall see the same battles, fought over the same phoney issues, all over again.
>
> There really is something deeply wrong . . . and I am not convinced that what is wrong is necessary tribulation about which nothing can be done.*

What is *deeply* wrong has to do with the absence of balance or wholeness in organizations, the bringing together of what is now split. In the terms used here you can label the split as being between Structural and Oceanic tendencies, or in Bateson's apt phrase, rigor and imagination. In the effort to bring about a wholeness, opposite tendencies often create conflict. When power becomes the goal of one side of the conflict, there can be no resolution. A new level of struggle must be reached where opposites are seen as complementary parts of the whole. Only leaders who personally embody the opposites within their own functioning will be able to bring organizations to this new level. There didn't seem to

* Reprinted from *Mind and Nature* by Gregory Bateson, p. 219, by permission of E. P. Dutton, Division of Elsevier-Dutton Publishing Co., Inc.

be enough of this kind of leadership around in the sixties in the churches and schools.

The schools experienced Oceanic protests that were at times explosive. Large numbers of people began seeing schooling as a box just as confining as the employment system we have been discussing. In the efforts made to escape the schooling box, extremes emerged that are worth examining from the perspective of the style compass.

Radical critics like Ivan Illich and Paulo Freire touched responsive chords with their criticisms of traditional forms of schooling. Illich insisted that compulsory education as developed in North America was wrong and had led to many social ills. While he negated what was going on, he had little to offer in the way of replacement and left despair hanging in the wake of his analysis. Freire analyzed the pedagogical process as oppressive, based on a master–slave relationship. A host of less radical critics joined in the chorus by calling for more freedom in the schools, while open classroom and organizational alternatives became popular solutions. The open classrooms became places where total freedom brought learning to a halt. All conception of authority and structure were lost in Oceanic reachings for the ultimate freedom. Caught in the same tendency to go to the extreme, alternative schools were often hopelessly disorganized, trying to reflect a bewildering range of viewpoints.

In all of these efforts there seemed to be very few leaders in the educational systems, capable of establishing a creative dialogue between the opposites involved. Instead lines were drawn between camps, doing little to enhance learning for those whom schools are supposed to be serving. Apparently, those in charge were unable to see the opposing forces as parts of a whole to be related to a *process* of development in which both sides are decreed as necessary. This will be a key for organization development in the eighties and a major lesson to be derived from the mistakes of the sixties in educational circles.

There were also eruptions within the various church organizations during the sixties. Perhaps the best example was Pope John XXIII, whose style was opposite to the leadership in Catholicism at that time. His simple, human presence and the decisions he made unleashed forces within individuals and organizations that had been neglected for too long. Again, there was the classic conflict between opposites. On the one side were the administrators responsible for the maintenance and smooth operation of a worldwide organization. Opposing their entrenched views was a new breed of theologians calling for reform in almost every aspect of the Catholic Church. In many ways the two groups needed each other—the managers required the vitality and creativity of the reformers, while the latter needed to appreciate the organizational implications of their suggestions. Unfortunately the leadership was, in this case too, not up to the task of relating to both sides effectively. A serious and sometimes damaging polarization took place that continues into the present. A similar polarization exists in other church groups around the issues of the ordination of women and the rights of homosexuals.

What can be learned from these experiences in educational and church organizations, what lessons for the eighties? First of all, these two organizations are signficant because they traditionally function as the sources of norms and values. When the institutions that are looked to as the communicators of norms are themselves in deep value conflicts, society has a special situation on its hands. In both settings, the functions of feeling and intuition, the combination creating the Oceanic style on our compass, have been the neglected functions. The leadership in both church and educational organizations tended to be weak in these functions. Persons strong in Oceanic tendencies frequently left the organizations. Vitality and growth in educational and religious institutions required the choice and vision that comes easy to the Oceanic style, but there was no effective dialogue with this feeling-intuitive side of things. Today neither the church nor the school seem to be the source of symbols and images around which we choose to organize our lives. The enthusiasm for change and hope for the future that was so intense in church and educational circles in the sixties has apparently diminished. Both settings are more than ever in need of vision and direction for basic changes, but they appear to lack the leadership. Will the same experience be true of organizations generally as we move through the next ten years?

YOUR PART IN THE FUTURE

All the old ways of thinking must be abandoned, if we are to develop the long-term strategies needed for the development of organizations where people spend their working lives. What Barbara Ward describes in her book *Progress for a Small Planet* as the "entirely inescapable physical interconnectedness of the planet which the human race must share if it is to survive" needs to become central in our thinking.* Work, everyone's work, must be effectively linked with this sense of interconnectedness. For this, you need before you a picture of the whole.

No matter where you are situated in an organization, whatever

* Barbara Ward, *Progress for a Small Planet* (New York: W. W. Norton and Co., 1979).

function you are involved in, it is possible to see your part in this struggle. When these connections are made, work takes on the meaning it originally had before specialization deprived us of a sense of the whole. Though it is impossible to return to the simplicity of a hunting society, it is possible to restore meaning to work by making this dual connection—your work is physically interconnected to the world and your work relates to your development.

In making this dual connection, you begin to see your part in the total scheme and thus participate in a process now necessary to the development of our planet. Career planning, if removed from this participation in the whole, can have no real meaning or long-term significance. When planning is done from such a perspective, there is the possibility of developing the leadership needed for the coming decade. Leaders will be capable of rising above conflicts and be able to bring opposing forces together for the development of the whole. The world can no longer afford the kind of "development" that is the result of one force overpowering another. In education and church organizations, just briefly described, there were unfortunately few people capable of guiding organizational processes toward the development of the whole. Instead organizations were and often continue to be divided by opposing viewpoints, so self-enclosed as to be blind to the needs of the whole. This will be the central issue in the eighties and must be carefully considered in any individual career planning.

The Call to the Individual—Moving Beyond the "Me Decade"

The changes necessary in the organizations that make up the world of work for most people will only come about through the efforts of the individual. The next decade requires leadership, at all levels of society, which will be willing to create the fundamentally new directions so far described. This kind of leadership will come from those who have faced internally the conflicts that now split organizations. Because they are unafraid of the opposites and capable of seeing the whole, they will be able to lead organizations. This is the basic call to individuals in every aspect of work: to rise above the pull of the status quo, to take control of their own work, and to renew the places of work generally. You can discover your own vocation in this fundamental need of society, and in being willing to meet the need you become involved in the true development of your personality. The "me decade" described by Tom Wolfe is over, and one conclusion that can be drawn from its aftermath is that there is little development of personality in the selfish pursuit of the isolated me. Development takes place in being involved in an inner call which involves us in the whole and its struggle for balance and completion.

In an essay concerning personality development, Jung defines vocation in these terms. Jung's work is based on his profound appreciation for the possibilities of adult development and is important in the effort to relate career to personal development. Making this connection is essential to the renewal of organizations in the eighties and enables career development to move beyond the concerns of the "me decade." Consider Jung's definition of vocation which he begins with a question.

> What is it, in the end, that induces a man to go his own way and to rise out of unconscious identity with the mass as out of a swathing mist? Not necessity, for necessity comes to many, and they all take refuge in convention. Not moral decision, for nine times out of ten we decide for convention likewise. What is it, then, that inexorably tips the scales in favour of the *extra-ordinary*?
>
> It is what is commonly called vocation: an irrational factor that destines a man to emancipate himself from the herd and from its well-worn paths. True personality is always a vocation and puts its trust in it as in God, despite its being, as the ordinary man would say, only a personal feeling. But vocation acts like a law of God from which there is no escape. The fact that many a man who goes his own way ends in ruin means nothing to one who has a vocation. He *must* obey his own law, as if it were a daemon whispering to him of new and wonderful paths. Anyone with a vocation hears the voice of the inner man: he *is called.**

Organizations in the eighties require the leadership of persons following this kind of inner call. When career can be related to such a call there is the possibility of restoring spirit to work and tackling the lack of inspiration that is at the heart of our productivity problems.

Two Crucial Polarities

In order to be able to dedicate yourself to work seen as related to your personal sense of vocation, two polarities will have to be met. The first has to do with man and woman within the nuclear family and the second with conservation and consumption. Let's look briefly at each.

* C. G. Jung, *Collected Works,* Vol. 17, pp. 175–176.

TRANSFORMING MALE/FEMALE ROLES

Women are here to stay in the work force and during the next decade they will be present in unprecedented numbers in organizations. This has enormous implications for the family as we have known it and requires a fundamental transformation of roles for both men and women. Clearly, women are being called to life-long careers and at the same time often remain called to motherhood. Men have got to change considerably to support this dual call and realize that they also have a dual responsibility. Previously, man's involvement in childrearing has been neglected and he has created an imbalance in his working life. This imbalance often surfaces cruelly at mid-career, when he realizes that his dreams for organizational success will not be realized and he has been a rotten father to boot. Very few are able to achieve what they expected in their careers, and this promises to be even more of a problem as we move into a decade of conservation and perhaps zero growth. As women aspire to both career and family they can lead men to more balanced lifestyles and both children and organizations will benefit. There is growing evidence that women involved in career pursuits experience considerable tension between job aspirations and desire for children and family. This tension or polarity can only be met through new forms of collaboration between men and women that will benefit both. As these issues are worked out, organizations stand to benefit considerably, so they should be involved through practical support immediately. Gone are the days when man or woman should be asked by an organization to sacrifice family to work. Just how an organization chooses to relate to this crucial polarity of the eighties will determine its degree of modernity or obsolescence.

MOVING FROM CONSUMPTION TO CONSERVATION

The second polarity relates to consumption and conservation. Most of us have been living a style of life based on consumption. With the worldwide energy crisis, we are now being forced toward very basic changes and a life based on conservation. As you saw earlier in this chapter, corporations must move toward conservation as a principle of action during the next decade. This move will only be possible if leadership emerges that has personally made the move. Simplification has to become a way of life for everyone in the Western world, and for this we have much to learn from the East. The great polarity of East and West on the planetary scale will be met during the eighties in this tension between consumption and conservation. Another way of seeing this issue is in the global struggle between the rich and poor nations, spoken about so strongly in the epigraph to this book. The rich nations must move from consuming most of the world's resources to a way of life based on conservation, and this will fundamentally transform organizations of all kinds. The movement will only be possible if it is led by individuals who have transformed their own lives in this regard. Because this polarity is so central to organizational life in the coming decade it is likewise central to career planning.

With the major organizational needs of the coming decade as background, consider how you can approach a specific function and industry to create a proposal that relates to these as well as more short-term needs.

ANALYZING INDUSTRY NEEDS

The development of a proposal is an effective way to study an industry in preparation for job search. The place to begin is with popular periodicals and newspapers reporting on developments in the industry. If you examine back issues of your best local paper and look through the last six months' issues of *Business Week, Forbes,* and *Fortune,* concentrating on all the industry-related articles, you will begin to get an overview of what's occurring. Also, you will begin to learn the language particular to that industry as you observe its professionals talking about their concerns. It pays to study this language, making sure you understand everything as you proceed. After a while you will notice things begin to get repetitive. It's like a circle closing around the industry as you fence it in with your research. At this point, it's time to proceed in your research by turning to those sources of information specially directed toward the industry.

If you contact the major associations related to the industry you're interested in, you will almost always be able to identify important publications—newsletters, journals, etc. The industry guides in the series related to this book list these associations as well as their publications. As you study these sources, you will be developing deeper knowledge of the industry and be able to identify its most pressing current problems as well as the developments that are accompanying these problems. As you do so, you can begin to select those of most interest to you and to which you bring special competence and experience. They should relate to your basic functional focus as discussed in Chapter 3. The problems thus selected are at the base of the proposal you can develop. An example here of the evolution of a proposal will be helpful.

Walter was, at 28, a successful manager of a large retail clothing store specializing in women's apparel. The store was the most important in a chain, but he didn't see much future in the family-owned operation and was feeling underemployed in the retail field. He had considerable writing ability, a keen intellect, good sales ability, and a real entrepreneurial spirit. His father had been a successful businessman, operating a number of small businesses.

Walt had entered retailing without much thought, after studying economics in college. He had strong intuitive ability and found marketing, especially new product development, to be an appropriate functional focus. An article in the *New York Times* business section on a new publishing venture attracted his attention one day. The article focused on a unique marketing strategy this new publishing company was planning to use in trying to sell its product. Basically, it involved using new retail outlets like department stores, supermarkets, and book stores to sell the encyclopedias with no reliance on door-to-door sales at all. The project struck Walt as interesting, since his knowledge of retailing would bring much to such an endeavor. He began reading generally about the publishing industry.

The popular press during the last few years had been talking a lot about the acquisition of publishing houses by a number of large conglomerates. He noticed that publishing professionals had mixed feelings about these acquisitions. Some saw them as providing impetus to the development of new markets for books; others felt the creativity and flexibility of the publishing company was threatened by the strict bottom-line orientation of big business. It was clear from these popular publications that the marketing of books was an area of considerable discussion in the publishing industry.

When he turned to the specialized industry publications, Walt began to get quite interested in the discussions being waged around new ways of marketing books. He put some ideas together about the encyclopedia project, seeing himself as capable of relating to retail outlets for the company, especially store managers in retail chains. He contacted the president of the encyclopedia publishing company and was referred to the Director of Marketing. He developed a brief proposal around his contacting store managers and called the Director of Marketing who asked him to send his proposal. He did so, but regretted it later. As a general rule, it is in your interest to meet about a proposal, not send your ideas through the mail. When he called the individual, he found him rather stand-offish and reluctant to explore the idea further. Basically, what he got was "we are already doing everything you say." Though the experience was a bit deflating, Walt continued pursuing the area of new marketing strategies for the publishing industry through industry publications.

In a newsletter from the Association of American Publishers, he learned about a seminar that was filled with ideas very like those he had presented on the encyclopedia project. He was also able to identify about seven professionals who were presenters at the seminar and their particular points of view. At this stage of his research, Walt began to zero in on the area of special sales in publishing. He began to investigate things like packaging and co-publishing, getting increasingly enthused about what he could bring to these activities from his retail experience. He got a specific idea for a co-publishing project involving retail clothing chains and a list of specialized publications that could be sold in these outlets. He now felt ready to approach a number of firms specializing in co-publishing projects. He found immediate receptivity for his ideas and a willingness to meet and discuss them.

In his third meeting, the president of a small, privately owned company told him how he started his company. It involved publishing a book on nutrition for babies, which he marketed through stores that carried baby clothes, toys, etc. It was so successful, he was able to create a new company on the basis of this item alone. He liked Walt, commented that he was just like him ten years ago and made him an interesting offer: He would back the development of a sample publication and pay Walt a nominal salary that would enable him to sell the project to large retail clothing chains. They would split the profits on the subsequent publishing project purchased by retailers. In effect, Walt had an opportunity to work with an experienced professional that could lead to launching his own venture in a few years. Armed with this offer, he decided to contact other companies, similarly involved in co-publishing projects. His search ended with accepting the original offer described above. Other opportunities appeared, but the chemistry with the president of the small company felt right. He was also attracted by the possibility of being on his own in a few years.

Walt's experience points up what an effective proposal makes possible in the way of designing a job search. First, the process of developing the proposal is a powerful method for analyzing the needs of an industry. By analyzing these needs in detail, you uncover information that professionals within the industry will value. This makes it much easier to establish contact with decision-makers in the industry. You have something to give them in the way of information, and this usually opens doors. Figure 22 presents a summary of the steps involved in proposal development and makes the method more explicit. There is a technique called "force field analysis" that entails identifying the driving forces in a particular field along with the trends that counter these forces. When thoroughly done, the development of a proposal as a self-marketing device provides you with both an overview of the industry and a specialized knowledge of its current needs. In a step-by-step procedure, this kind of analysis leads to the isolation of the most important forces and coun-

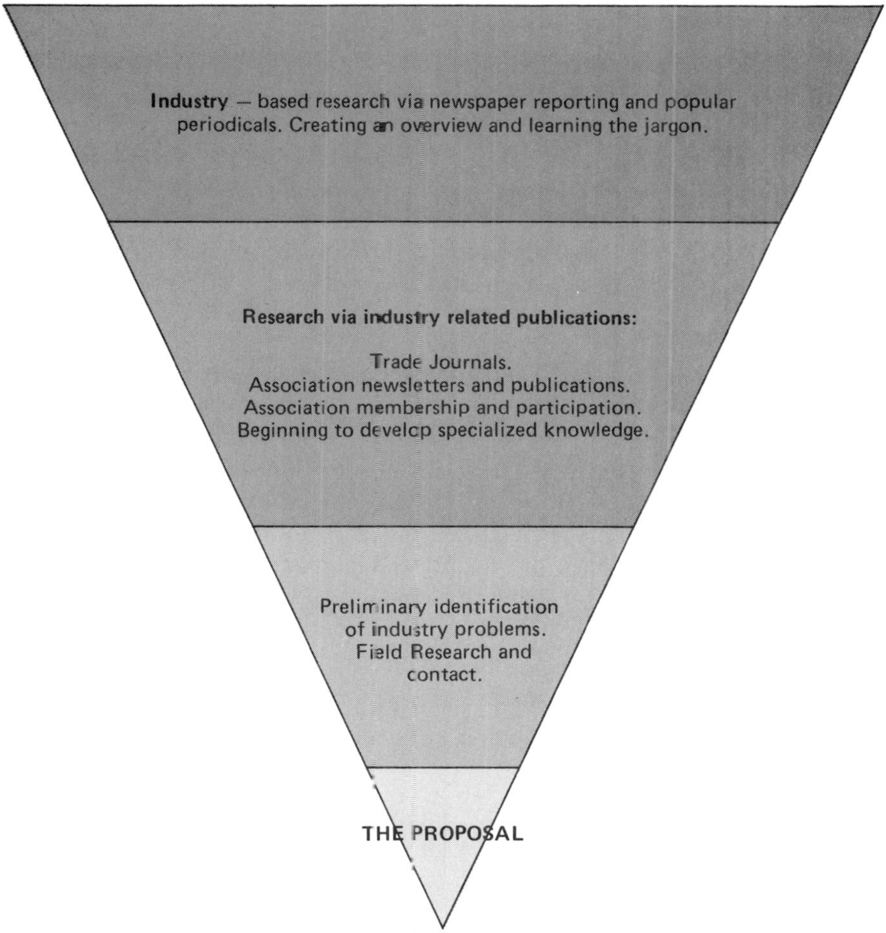

Industry — based research via newspaper reporting and popular periodicals. Creating an overview and learning the jargon.

Research via industry related publications:

Trade Journals.
Association newsletters and publications.
Association membership and participation.
Beginning to develop specialized knowledge.

Preliminary identification of industry problems. Field Research and contact.

THE PROPOSAL

FIGURE 22 Developing a Proposal in Preparation for Job Search—Industry Research.

terforces in the field, enabling decisions to be made in regard to action. Figure 22 tries to show how such an analysis likewise occurs as you research an industry for the purpose of creating proposals.

It would be well to relate Walter's project to the more global concerns described earlier. For the first time since college he felt enthused about an idea and a project that was truly his own. Whatever effort he put in would produce results that were his, and he was free of the discomfort of being used strictly for the purposes of others. The size of the project was such that he could see it through from start to finish. He found a greater amount of flexibility and openness in the small publishing companies, and though he received consistent support for the idea behind his proposal, the professionals in the large firms often had a "but" to add to their expression of support for the idea. Usually this reservation had to do with general company policy on which they felt blocked. For his own long-term satisfaction, it looked like the smaller company was the way to go. It also provided a path to his own business, assuming a few years of successful experience in the industry.

Many of the issues related to the old and the new laws of corporate development are illustrated by Walt's experience. His own productivity and motivation were greatly enhanced when he began reaping the fruits of his own work. The size of an organization alone need not be a negative factor when it comes to creativity and the ability to respond to new ideas. Size must be controlled in relation to giving people direct contact with what they produce and some type of ownership. In this experience, company size did seem to be a factor and Walt found a severe conservatism in some of the large publishing companies when it came to new product development and marketing strategies. He noticed an over-reliance on numbers and a fear of reprisals from above if a proposal wasn't a sure thing.

SUMMARY

In this chapter you have seen the major needs of organizations for the eighties. Around these needs most of the changes in organizations will take place and employment opportunities will be connected to these changes. At the present moment, it is possible to create intelligent proposals related to these various needs in order to develop your own career opportunities.

The next chapter will describe how to use the proposal in conducting a systematic job search.

REFRAMING THE JOB SEARCH: NETWORKING

PURPOSE

Is there a practical and creative way of doing a job search for someone committed to personal control over his own career? Yes, there is a method. It requires time, hard work, and observance of principles, but it takes you out of the framework in which you are merely fitted into a job slot or seen as a function. Learning the method will involve some second-order change, so be prepared to shake loose from your old ways of thinking about job hunting.

As you confront the employment system, significant personal changes need to be made which involve altering those internal mental frames you bring to the process of finding a job. We have briefly discussed these changes in Chapter 1. Here we will describe in detail the specific nature of the changes required. We begin by looking at traditional approaches to job search in order to fully appreciate their limitations.

TRADITIONAL APPROACHES TO THE JOB SEARCH

Most people looking for a job use some or all of the following strategies:

1. Preparing a résumé.
2. Registering with employment agencies.
3. Monitoring the newspapers for positions wanted and sending résumés to those announced.
4. Sending unsolicited résumés to personally selected companies.
5. Going to personnel departments and filling out applications.
6. Asking personal acquaintances for their assistance.

These strategies constitute about 90 percent of job-search activities. They do, in fact, lead to employment for many people. And yet these strategies are severely limited because they in no way reach the hidden job market. This hidden market contains most of the better job opportunities. When you reframe your approach to the employment system, you increase your chances of reaching this mainstream of employment activity.

Let us conduct an exercise in reframing. Spend several moments looking at the picture in Figure 23, then describe what you see.

FIGURE 23 An Exercise in Reframing.

The image, you may have discovered, is ambiguous. It actually contains two possible meanings. From one perspective you see a cup or a chalice. From another perspective you see two faces looking at one another. If at first you only see a chalice, by reframing you can change the meaning of the picture into two faces. The reframing is accomplished by taking the white portion of the picture and visually pushing it into the background. When this is accomplished, the black immediately becomes the front or foreground. A similar reframing is important as you view the employment system. You need to push your mental frames about how the system works and how you seek a job into the background. Once this is accomplished, you have taken the first step in the reframing process.

Tom Jackson and Davidyne Mayleas in their book *The Hidden Job Market* (New York: Quadrangle, 1976) give one of the better analyses of how the system works. The bottom line is that most employment opportunities remain hidden or informal. What becomes formally visible is a minimal part of the available opportunities. Most employment activity occurs in a hidden job market that becomes accessible only when you reframe your approach to job hunting.

A job becomes formally visible in several ways; by being advertised; placed with an agency; or given to the personnel department within companies. These opportunities constitute approximately 25 to 35 percent of currently available jobs (see Figure 24).

The employment system continues to operate in this fashion despite the changes brought about by affirmative action legislation, which demands that more information be published. The growing practice of posting all job opportunities within major corporations, or advertising positions in educational and government establishments has not substantially altered how people are employed.

FIGURE 24 Sources of Employment Activity.

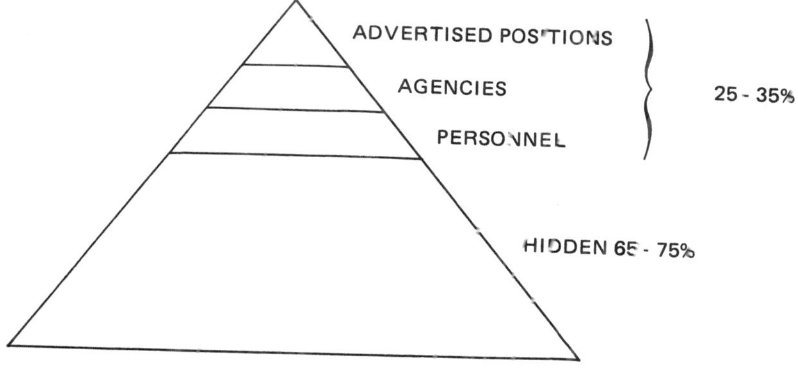

An example will illustrate how the system most often works. Ted is a research microbiologist who was seeking employment within the Environmental Protection Agency (EPA). By developing an extensive network of contacts he managed to gain access to the director of the group within the EPA for which he wanted to work. There were two openings available, neither of which had yet been advertised. By the end of his first meeting with the director, Ted was verbally assured of one of these positions, despite the fact that Ted had not yet registered with Civil Service, an absolute necessity for government employment. The director assured Ted that lack of registration was a minor obstacle. All Ted needed to do was get registered, and he (the director) would do the rest. The director then arranged to have Ted placed in the appropriate registration level. To by-pass those who were ahead of Ted on the Civil Service registry, the director interviewed some applicants whom he found "inadequate" and described the job to others in a way that made it impossible for them to accept. Ted went to work one month later.

Similar processes happen daily despite jobs becoming formally visible. In education for example, where positions by law must be advertised, many of the jobs are filled informally, frequently before they are advertised. At times, committees interview would-be employees even though the job has already been filled.

The same process takes place in corporations despite new posting procedures. People are often offered a position and at the same time informed it will be three weeks before they can officially go on the payroll because the posting and interviewing procedures must be followed.

These examples are cited to show how opportunities formally made visible through advertising or posting are frequently already filled. To understand and accept that this is the system is the beginning of the reframing process. Let's examine more closely the traditional methods for doing a job search.

Mailing Résumés to advertised positions does work for some people. It is effective if: the résumé is well done, the candidate has impressive experience in the field, and if the advertised position still exists. Just plain luck in the paper shuffle that transpires when the employer decides whom to interview, is also a factor.

Advertised positions often elicit hundreds of résumés. Employers who get exhausted sorting through the paper, at times overlook the best candidates. To avoid the paper mess and the resulting inefficiency, the process of advertising and sorting is frequently bypassed.

The director of corporate communications of a major company in the data processing industry told this story about hiring a copywriter. He began by calling his own contacts to see if any were aware of copywriters looking for work. This took two days and resulted in no referrals. He then contacted an executive search firm that specialized in copywriters. The search firm sent him ten résumés. In reviewing the résumés, none of the candidates looked satisfactory. The process had now taken over ten days. In "desperation," since he needed the person immediately, he placed an ad in the *New York Times,* describing the job, gave the company name, and asked applicants to send résumés. Two weeks later he had received 675 résumés with cover letters, and one lone letter with no résumé. After sorting through the papers, he selected six people to interview, one being the author of the letter with no résumé. After seeing the candidates, he decided to hire the individual who had sent the lone cover letter. The entire process took the director six weeks. The final irony occurred two weeks later when a bill arrived from the search agency announcing that the person hired had been referred by them. As it turned out the new employee's résumé had been one of the ten originally sent by the agency and rejected by the director.

This incident illustrates not only the ineffectiveness of résumés, but also the lack of efficiency in the entire hiring process.

Unsolicited Résumés directed to specific people within an organization are usually forwarded to personnel. Many job seekers could paper their walls with the courteous form letters from personnel departments which say in effect "thank you for your interest, we'll keep you on file." As a general rule, therefore, when seeking employment for an unadvertised position, *never lead with a résumé.*

Using your Friends to help you get a position is fraught with problems. The major difficulty in this approach is that frequently awkward interpersonal situations are created. This is especially true when you are not clear about your objectives.

A case in point is Jim who asked his brother-in-law, president of a small management consulting firm, for assistance in getting a job. In his approach, Jim was not clear about what kind of work he wanted or where he wanted to work. In effect, he was asking his brother-in-law to take responsibility for deciding where and what Jim should do and then for introducing him to the appropriate people. No one in his right mind, let alone a brother-in-law, would take on such responsibility. Assuming that he could make the right connections and help Jim secure a position, the unknown future consequences would be sufficient reason to avoid helping. The emotional conflict the brother-in-law experienced made it difficult for him to choose between feelings of loyalty to family and loyalty to his connections where his professional reputation was on the line.

Using Agencies presents a job searcher with several choices.

1. The Employment Agency seeks to learn about available positions from client companies and then fits individuals into these available jobs. Their

major concern is to satisfy the client company; they are not organized to assist individuals making a change, and they have access to only a limited part of the real market. Usually their listings are of lower level jobs.

2. The Executive Search firm is hired by a company to fill a specific position, usually at a high level, within the client company. The search firm usually contacts individuals, since their habitual mode of operation is to hunt out persons already in positions that fit the request of their client. They are therefore not highly effective for unemployed people.
3. The Placement Office specializes in a particular field, or it might be university/college based. It places those on file into positions that are made known to them by specific employers. Its drawback is limited access to real opportunities.
4. Career Consulting or Counseling Firms work for individuals by helping them identify objectives and organize and execute job searches. The services are essentially counseling and aid by way of instruction and information for job search. The fees are paid by the individual. The limitation of such agencies are related to the quality of counseling one receives and the substance of the information provided in the job search phase.

The job searcher who accepts how the employment system operates begins to put the traditional approaches in perspective. Not more than 25 to 35 percent of your energies should be put into such methods. The remaining energy should go into other strategies.

REFRAMING YOUR APPROACH

Another internal change is necessary before maximum job search efficiency is possible. This change has to do with your approach to the employment system—the attitude you have about what you seek. A common attitude can be accurately described as "begging." You attempt to discover the available slots or positions, and "beg" to be fitted into the one which pinches least. There is a better option available. First find out whether the job is what you want and then interview the employer. It is important to realize that assuming this posture is not just a technique. It demands a fundamental change in attitude. Your attitude has to be based on a certainty about what you want from your work and in your ability to get what you want. You are in control. Only when your attitude toward the employment system has been reframed in this complete way are you ready to increase your effectiveness through personal contacts. Since most job opportunities remain hidden, it is imperative to be connected to the network of people who are sources or channels of employment information you need to meet your objectives. Developing these relationships is the heart of becoming part of the significant network of professionals related to these objectives. Achieving this participation is called *networking*.

How Accessible Are People?

Most business executives are relatively accessible, a phenomenon neither understood nor utilized by most job seekers. The following exercise illustrates this point.

Assume, for a moment, you have a personal message to be delivered to the President of the United States. You may only take that message to someone that you personally know. The person to whom you take the note must then take it to someone he personally knows. Try to guess the number of moves necessary to have the message reach the President.

Most people could accomplish this task within five moves. (Lawyer, Mayor, State Senator, Senator, Cabinet member.) If you realize that the President of the United States can be reached this easily, you can appreciate the accessibility of other people. It is by knowing accessible and appropriate people that active networking begins. To use this system successfully, it is first necessary to understand the nature of networks.

A *network* is a structure of relationships through which information and ideas flow in constant motion. At the same time, every network is defined by some common factor. None exists without the activity, whether conscious or unconscious, of at least two people. Some are quite formal and regulated, such as professional associations or trade groups. Other networks are equally valid, but quite informal. But even the most formal ones change from day to day. This afternoon's American Medical Association differs subtly from yesterday's, and quite markedly from last year's. The intended or formal structure is probably the same, but the informal structure—who is really responsible for doing what—is different.

Networks are found in every sphere of human activity. Every person exists as a member of many networks, from family to college to club to community, and so on. The idea of networks is not new or radical, but for all their ubiquity, the consciousness of them is amazingly rare. Many people are champion "networkers," regularly contributing to, developing, and benefiting from hundreds of them, but would not be aware of any of this activity as something planned or intended. They may say something, like, "I just know a lot of people," which, while probably true, is hardly descriptive of the dynamics of what they are doing. Consciousness of networks is the first step for the job searcher. And to become conscious of networks, you must recognize one when you see one.

RECOGNITION OF NETWORKS

All networks, formal or informal, exist for some common purpose. They can be defined by that purpose and, hence, can be recognized by working backwards from their goals. Every network can be categorized as a group of people interested in or involved (consciously or not) in a common goal. The goal of increased sales of Product A defines a network. Its members will span many activities, firms, associations, clubs, groups, and job titles. Most of them will only be aware of parts of the network, but the larger network exists and links them all. If you feel that you have something to contribute to increased sales of Product A, the breadth of the network you define is going to determine in large part how successful you are in joining the common effort in a meaningful way.

A simple example is to consider all the people whose goal is to arrive in the city from the suburbs at approximately 8:15 A.M. Together they constitute an informal network. Most of them don't know one another. They have no collective bylaws, no constitution. They don't even know how many of them there are—very informal. Within this larger network are a variety of smaller ones:

those who make the trip by automobile
those who take the bus
those who ride the train

Within these sub-sets the organization and consciousness of the network becomes considerably clearer. The train riders, for example, can be divided into two or three train loads. Each train load can be broken down into different cars. The members of these sub-networks tend to at least see one another and—a critical point at this level—the members are able to communicate. Contact can be made with fellow network members. At this stage, the ability to communicate permits the formal organization or use of the network for mutual benefit. A model of conscious identification and use of a network might operate like this:

> A new resident of the suburbs decides that he needs to get to the city at 8:15 every morning, but on a limited budget. He seeks information on the means available and makes some preliminary decisions:

automobile travel is too expensive and, anyway, the car's needed at home

the bus schedule is inconvenient, but marginally acceptable

the train schedule is good, but involves using the car to get to the station.

His new goal becomes organizing a carpool from his neighborhood to the station so that he can use the train but minimize the use of his car. An intermediate goal is the identification of those people in his neighborhood who use the train. To do this he begins to ride the train every day and makes contact with those fellow commuters he has identified as driving from his neighborhood. By leaving home at different times and taking several routes, he is able to follow several people to the station parking lot, introduce himself, and propose a share-the-ride arrangement.

While the commuter in this example didn't need any consciousness of networks or network building, his activities illustrate the basic steps in the productive use of a network:

identification of goals	a carpool
identification of the basic network	commuters using the train
identification of members of the network most likely to share goals	commuters from the neighborhood
planning and arranging contact with these members	following drivers to lot
making contact	introducing self
making specific proposal	suggesting carpool

Let us now examine these phases of network use in more detail.

PHASES OF NETWORKING

There are, in general, two major activities—the identification of an appropriate network and its members, and the conscious interaction with it. In a word, networking.

Identification Phase

IDENTIFYING SPECIFIC GOALS

Identifying specific goals is the first step in the process of job seeking using the networking method. Since network development will require some energy, specific goals will help you to conserve and channel your energy more efficiently. Too broad a career goal leads to diffusion of energy and tends to keep you at too general a level, instead of at the focused, specific level where real results can take place.

If you have several goals and do not feel ready to choose among them, it is better to pursue one than to start exploring all of them at once. Actively relating to the network will help clarify interests and values, and hence, define your career goals more precisely.

As stated before, the networks are there—formal, informal, broad, or narrow—they exist and need only conscious linkage to become functioning entities. The first step in identifying networks is to gather information related to your goals. This first step is crucial; its importance cannot be overemphasized. The more you put into researching the function and industry related to your goal, the more efficient your search will be. The industry guides of this series are designed to give you the necessary information to begin your personal research.

Besides the information in the Guides, you must be alert to new and ever changing sources of information. Most articles in leading business periodicals (like *Business Week, Fortune,* and *Forbes*) usually refer to many people who were interviewed by the reporter; in many cases their organizational affiliation and title are also supplied. This is the most current information about your objective. Brief articles may have taken the reporter months to research, and intelligent job searchers, conserving energy, will utilize all such information.

How to read sources is also very important. As an illustration, read the following article which appeared in *Business Week* (February 26, 1979).* Assume that your broad career goal is to *enter the personnel field* and that you are beginning to prepare for a job search. As you read the article, note the names, titles, and affiliations of people that could be useful in your job search.

Personnel Widens Its Franchise

Until three years ago, the personnel department at Standard Brands Inc. was virtually indistinguishable from those that have existed since the dawn of the corporate era. Composed of a director of labor relations and a director of benefits—each with a salary in the $30,000 range—and a staff of about 20, the department routinely administered hiring and firing procedures, handled labor negotiations, maintained employee records, administered benefits, and saw to it that paychecks went out on time. Its decisions could vitally affect individual employees, but they had little impact on the direction of the corporation, and the department was buried well below finance, marketing, and planning in the corporate bureaucracy.

The old personnel staff is still performing many of the same functions at Standard Brands today, but now it is part of a new human resources department, four times the size of the original personnel department and headed up by a corporate vice-president, Madelyn P. Jennings, whose salary and responsibilities are easily double those of the two directors combined. Part of that growth is the result of a flood of new government regulations that have increased the importance and the complexity of traditional personnel administration tasks. Since joining the company in 1976, Jennings has instituted a national compensation program, overhauled benefits, and developed an employee appraisal system.

But much of the stunning growth of Jennings' department is the result of a brand-new role that has been assigned to personnel administration at Standard Brands: the development and implementation of the company's first manpower planning system, one that is directly tied to carrying out corporate strategies. This new personnel function at Standard Brands is typical of similar changes taking place in most other large corporations that promise to lift top personnel administrators, who increasingly are adopting the human resources designation, into prominence as powerful officers in the corporate hierarchy. Already, experts estimate, such human resources executives—whether they carry the title or not—now hold key manpower planning responsibilities in almost all of the nation's 500 largest industrial companies, compared with only a handful of companies five years ago.

Hired by CEOs. While their staffs still handle such mundane chores as allocating spaces in the company parking lot, they are also expected to work closely with senior operating managers to create staffing plans that are designed to meet corporate goals and to satisfy the growing demands by employees for clear career paths they can follow. "Management realizes that its important assets are not simply financial resources but having the people on hand at the right time and in the right place to make a thing go," observes Thomas C. Stevens, who in 1974 filled a new post as corporate director of human resources at J. I. Case Co., the construction and farm equipment subsidiary of Tenneco Inc.

Not surprisingly, personnel executives able to tackle such herculean tasks are commanding top dollar. A recent study by Heidrick & Struggles Inc., a Chicago-based executive-search firm, shows that the average salary of senior human resources executives is $79,000, compared with $52,000 for personnel executives who normally do not perform manpower planning. Even senior personnel executives who may handle human resources responsibilities but do not have the title average $61,000. And one human resources officer recently told *Business Week* that, counting performance incentives, his annual compensation can top $250,000. "Today corporations recognize that the right executive in human resources can add to profits," comments Lester B. Korn, president of Korn/Ferry International, an executive-search firm that conducted 28 searches for human resources vice-presidents in the last two years, a 30% increase from the prior two years.

Pipeline to the Top. Chief executive officers are increasingly taking an active role in such searches, a clear indication that the human resources position is gaining importance. Standard Brands' Jennings recalls one prehiring interview with F. Ross Johnson, the company's chairman, that lasted seven hours. William M. Buck Jr., who holds the new post of senior vice-president of human resources at Peabody Coal Co., was hired by President and Chief Executive Officer Robert H. Quenon. And at American Express Co., Chairman James D. Robinson III and President Roger H. Morley insisted on interviewing all potential candidates for the job themselves before hiring Philip H. Prince last August as AmEx's senior vice-president for personnel and management development.

The pipeline to the top rarely stops after hiring. Many human resources executives such as Buck report directly to the CEO. Others—Jennings is one—sit on corporate policy committees. "More and more, key human resources people are sitting at the CEO's right elbow," notes Gerard R. Roche, president of Heidrick & Struggles.

Tenneco is typical of the trend to relate manpower planning to corporate goals and strategies. The company recently started requiring vice-presidents to submit a five-year "executive resources" projection along with their five-year business plans. Both are closely reviewed by Kenneth L. Otto, senior vice-president of employee relations, who determines if they are compatible. If a division, for example, is planning to shift from a marketing to a production orientation, Otto must make certain that it is planning not only to develop a large enough production staff to meet the new demands in that area but also to make a suitable reduction of marketing specialists. "We're looking at how people figure into the equation as a long-range problem," says Otto.

Development Goals. Such planning is essential for companies with ambitious growth goals. AmEx, for example, has plans to expand into new business areas that will double its employee population to 70,000 over the next ten years. Even without this growth, the company's annual turnover rate produces a need for more than 500 new people a year. As a result, a manager's performance will be judged on how well he has been able to grow people in his own organization, and up to 10% of an executive's bonus could be negatively affected for failure to meet management development goals. That, in turn, is already placing a heavy demand on Personnel Senior Vice-President Prince to develop new programs to teach AmEx executives necessary skills in employee recruitment, training, and career counseling.

The new stress on human resources planning has resulted in a major expansion in the entire area of personnel, and experts estimate that the number of specialists in the field has doubled in the last five years. At Hibernia Bank, in San Francisco, Max H. Forster, the new vice-president and director of personnel, more than doubled the size of his unit from 6 to 14 people in only six months. At Levi Strauss & Co., Harold M. Goldstein, director of employee selection and development, recently was authorized to hire human resources staffers "at a time when we were trying as a company to hold the line."

Unlike its predecessors in personnel, who thought mostly in terms of answering or silencing employee complaints, the new breed of human resources executives focuses much more sharply on profits. That often means reorienting personnel staffs toward a bottom-line view that once seemed alien to them. Laurence E. Mullen recalls that when he became vice-president of personnel and organization at Allegheny Ludlum Industries Inc., in 1974, his staff "not only lacked awareness of how they could impact the profitability of a business, but they weren't aware that people wanted them to." Mullen's solution: A series of intensive training seminars in corporate finance were given to the company's entire personnel staff.

Way Station. Luckily, corporations are starting to get an influx of people with both an interest in human resources and a thorough grounding in business. In many companies, personnel was once considered a dumping ground for executives who could not succeed in running operating divisions. More common now are executives such as James W. Kennedy, manager of human resources planning and employment for General Foods Corp., who switched careers after 12 years as a successful marketing executive. Also typical are a growing number of line managers who believe that two- to three-year stints as human resources executives can be a major way station in their route to the top. And they can point to a lengthening list of examples to support that belief, including W. Thomas Beebe, chairman of Delta Airlines Inc., and J. Stanford Smith, chairman of International Paper Co., both of whom spent time as personnel executives.

Business schools are accommodating this trend by turning out more MBAs who believe that human resources is where the action is. "Since 1975, we've had a 50% increase in the number of graduates who are interested in this position," comments J. Frederic Way, associate dean of placement and career services at Columbia University's Graduate School of Business. Similarly, Frank H. Cassell, professor of industrial relations at Northwestern University's Graduate School of Management, watched attendance at his seminar for human resources soar from only six students eight years ago to 275 students this year—roughly 80% of the entire graduating class. And at the University of Pennsylvania's Wharton School of Business, three to five students each semester are taking independent majors in human resources, majors that were not even provided five years ago.

While a variety of factors explain the growing role of corporate human resources departments, the one most commonly cited is government. Dozens of new federal laws— from the Employee Retirement Income Security Act to the Equal Employment Opportunity Act—spell out how companies must treat existing and prospective employees, and compliance often involves expensive new programs. Peabody Coal's human resources department, for example, began supervising a program costing more than $500,000 in 1973 that simulates various mining conditions in order to train some 15,000 miners a year—all to ensure compliance with the Mining Safety & Health Act. And Standard Brands' Jennings notes that the number of statutes enforced by the Labor Dept. has increased from 40 in 1960 to 130 now.

A less obvious but equally important reason for the closer attention large companies are giving to human resources is the skyrocketing cost of employee benefits, which has risen from just above 20% of an average employee's salary five years ago to 35% today. With so much invested in an employee, reducing turnover rates is crucial. At Tenneco's J. I. Case subsidiary, the human resources department is credited with helping the company reduce its monthly turnover rate to 1.1%, compared with an industry average of 1.5% a month, by developing clearer job performance criteria and better training programs and by emphasizing promotion from within.

Thanks to a new system for spotting and tracking internal managerial talent, Case fills 80% of its salaried slots with insiders, up from 50% five years ago.

The Payoff. Yet human resources executives are by no means over all of the hurdles in establishing their new role in the corporation. The problem of putting manpower training programs in place and "getting management to buy them" still remains, observes Ruben Krigsman, manager of personnel research at Union Carbide Corp. But he notes that a "new breed" of operating managers is coming along who show far more respect for personnel executives. Five years ago, Krigsman figures, he initiated 90% of all of his contacts with top management. Now they come to him about 60% of the time.

One major reason for that, says Krigsman, is that top management increasingly appreciates the profit potential of human resources executives. To illustrate, he recalls how in 1976 he was dispatched to Carbide's Pleasantville (N.Y.) plant to try to boost employee productivity and morale. After running various surveys, Krigsman instituted new training programs and reorganized the workplace to give blue-collar workers more responsibile jobs. In just three months, productivity soared by 25%; the amount of finished goods passing inspection jumped from 60% to 80%; and absenteeism dropped from 5% to 3%. As a result of such triumphs in human resources management, says Krigsman, "managers recognize that there's a payoff for both the business and the employees."

The article you just read contains the following information. See if you noted all of it in your initial reading.

Organizations	People
Standard Brands, Inc.	Madelyn P. Jennings, Corporate Vice President, Human Resources
J. I. Case Company Subsidiary Tenneco, Inc.	Thomas C. Stevens, Corporate Director, Human Resources
Tenneco	Kenneth L. Otto, Senior Vice President, Employee Relations
Heidrick & Struggles, Inc. (executive search firm)	Gerard R. Roche, President
Korn/Ferry (executive search firm)	Lester B. Korn
Peabody Coal Co.	William M. Buck, Jr., Senior Vice President, Human Resources
American Express	Phillip H. Prince, Senior Vice President, Personnel
Hibernia Bank	Max H. Forster, Vice President, Personnel
Levi Strauss & Co.	Harold M. Goldstein, Director, Employee Selection

Organizations	People
Allegheny Ludlum Industries, Inc.	Laurence E. Mullen, Vice President, Personnel
General Foods	James W. Kennedy, Manager, Human Resource Planning
Union Carbide Corp.	Ruben Krigsman, Manager, Personnel Research

This was the most up-to-date information available at the time it was published. Interestingly, even this information needed to be checked because of the speed with which change occurs. For example, James Kennedy of General Foods who is mentioned in the article had changed jobs only weeks after publication, becoming head of Human Resources at J. Walter Thompson.

IDENTIFYING MEMBERS

Identifying members of the network who are likely to share your goals is a direct continuation of the general research. As you begin to perceive the general layout of your field of interest, you should begin to use more and more specific tools. Here the sections on Associations and the Directory portion of the Guides should come into play.

Every industry or field has its own *Directories.* These valuable tools contain the names and addresses of all key personnel in the organizations within your field of interest. Some directories may be difficult to find in public libraries, therefore you need to identify the special libraries around the country which contain specific industry-related materials.

Besides directories, *associations* are central sources of information. These groups exist to promote the interests of their members and frequently serve as clearing houses for information for their members. Because of their purpose, essentially one of public relations, these groups are easily accessible. Some provide placement services and most have contact with their active members, therefore they can refer you to others in the association network. In this stage of networking, your object is to identify those organizations, firms, and people who are likely to share your interests and who participate in the network you want to join. An openness about possible members is important. If some turn out to be unrelated there should be a ready reserve of candidates to continue your sorting process. Remember that the explicit connection of a person to a network (e.g., a member of a professional association) is only one facet of your search. There are equally valid tangential connections. For example, a member of an organization which is peripheral to your field of interest, but whose role in the organization is directly related to the kind of job you want. As an illustration, if you are interested in public relations you should consider not only explicitly PR-related groups, but people in other groups who work indirectly with PR people or groups. For this reason we have included, when possible, listings of functionally related associations in the section on associations in each Guide in the present series.

As the preliminary identification of your network nears its conclusion, you should have a good idea of where many of the potential members can be found. When you feel the network is broad enough, you should start to interact with its members. But be sure to continue the identification phase. You will soon be gathering more and better information. This will provide more specifically related contacts for your list of potential network members, as well as more information about the concerns and trends in the field of your interest.

Active Networking

The information from the Guides in this series, as well as that you have assembled yourself, will prepare you to start active networking. It can be an interesting, exciting, and very useful experience. First, some general notes on the principles of networking that are crucial to its success. The development and use of a network is a form of self-help, but it must be more than that to be of real value or effectiveness. You are going to meet and interact with a variety of people whose primary goals in life are not, after all, to assist you in achieving yours. You are going to ask them for their time, attention, thoughts, opinions, reactions, ideas. You are going to ask them to identify associates and colleagues. Fair play demands that you give them something in return. The network is not designed for taking or for self-aggrandizement. In its most effective form it is an organization for sharing. It has to be. Its energy and power are derived from the shared goals and coordinated interactions of a group of complex individuals. Reciprocity is the only lubricant that can keep it from grinding to a halt.

We cannot emphasize this point of reciprocity too strongly. You need to break out of the "begging frame" of traditional job seekers. When you begin to freely *give* to the network, rather than only *take,* networking will be most fruitful. Let your principle be "*gifting.*" What am I going to give Mrs. X during this meeting? With such a frame you will be capable of having a reciprocal exchange which is useful for both parties.

It is at this initial stage of active contact that many novice networkers begin to hesitate. Take the steps one by one and follow through to actual contact. See what happens. Learn from the experiences, but act—it is the only cure for a very natural feeling of uncertainty and inertia. And remember that as you proceed, as you learn more, you will have more and more to offer. You will become a resource and, in many cases, an expert overview person precisely because you will be doing what many people would like to do but never manage to accomplish.

If you have reframed, initial anxieties are lessened. Simply reflect on the difference between having to ask for something (beg) and giving something. Begging generates anxiety and fear, gifting creates feelings of ease. As a beginning networker you can gift other members with overview information as well as fresh insight and enthusiasm.

After viewing the network research you have accomplished, sketch out a rough map of who should be contacted and in what order. Have several potential contacts for each stage in case any are unresponsive or turn out to be inappropriate.

Your early efforts should be directed at the more broadly based organizations in the specific industry you are targeting. Your early contact will be necessarily general until you are better informed. By the time you approach people very closely in tune with your ultimate goal, you want to be as prepared as possible. You also want to represent the range of contacts already made so that your visibility in the field will add depth to what you can provide to the ultimate contacts. Remember your map is a flexible guideline, to be modified as new information and new contacts are generated.

As you begin networking, you should be constantly aware of the two goals that form the basis of this active phase.

1. You need to become informed about every aspect of your primary area of interest—the trends, needs, issues, facts, and figures.
2. You need to become visible within this network so that your interests, abilities, and energies are known and can be drawn upon or recommended to others.

Your goal will be much more easily attained if you are well informed and if the right people have met you and are aware of your interests, goals, and knowledge. You will meet many people, but for successful meetings, you must give as well as receive. By usng this process, with an emphasis on sharing, you will increase your efficiency several hundred percent.

Personal Network Identification

Before beginning to interact with the new network, you should spend several hours creating a list of everyone involved in your personal network, that is, everyone you have come to know personally during your adult life. This list will consist of people you can telephone directly and set up a time to meet. The purpose of such meetings will be to inform these people of your objectives. It is highly probable that they will know someone who could introduce you to people directly connected to the new network you wish to enter or at least indirectly related to this group. Remember the exercise of delivering a message to the president of the United States. The same principle will work: your personal network will directly introduce you to your new targeted network.

Old Frames In New Disguises

As you begin to interact with the network, there are experiences which can reveal whether or not you have really reframed your approach. In the following story, did reframing really take place?

Barbara was a music teacher who began networking in order to enter the recording industry. One of her first active contacts was with the director of an association serving recording companies. The theoretical intent of the meeting was to interview the director about the nature of the association's work, current issues and concerns of record companies, and possible names of other people with whom she should speak. During the actual interview these were some of the questions that Barbara asked:

> What are the opportunities for someone like me?
> Are record companies employing people (like me) today?
> Are you aware of any companies looking for people (like me)?
> How do I begin?
> Who should I see?

The entire meeting centered on Barbara (I, me). It lasted fifteen minutes and resulted in no referrals and little information.

Contrast this with the experience of Samuel, an ex-minister, who began active networking with the director of an association serving sales executives. Sam's objective: a position as staff assistant in international marketing. The interview lasted two-and-a-half hours and centered on issues in international marketing, as well as techniques for job search. The meeting resulted in Sam's being invited to several meetings of the association's placement committee. Further, Sam volunteered to give a class for a society member at a local college. The end result was that the director personally introduced Sam to the V.P. of International

Marketing of a major corporation which effectively developed his network.

EFFECTIVE NETWORKING

In networking, your communications with contacts must always be direct, truthful, and straightforward. Deceptive practices or evasive statements will only impede your progress. If you need information, ask for it, explain why you want it, and try to be precise. Most executives are understandably reluctant to spend time on generalities with people who haven't done their homework. Try to establish your credibility through the presentation or discussion of relevant specific issues. This will separate you from the casual inquirer.

Make it easy for the contact. If you seek a written reply, provide a self-addressed, stamped envelope. If you want an interview or meeting, do the telephoning and arranging around your contact's schedule.

It is important to reiterate that networking interviews are not job interviews. Although the contact knows that you are looking for employment eventually, you should let him know that this meeting has a purpose other than direct job solicitation. The purpose of all networking interviews is to provide you a way of relating to the professionals in your field of interest. The emphasis is on *relating, participating;* not on soliciting positions.

After contacting formal organizations, review your findings and move on to more individuals, always expanding the network, always contributing what you can. A good networker becomes a cross-pollinator of contacts and ideas. As you gain more information, your focus should become sharper and your meetings more effective. But make a conscious effort to come to the point. General information builds a framework, but hard facts fill it out and make it functional. So prepare yourself for an expedition into learning and sharing that will empower both you and every member of your network. Make things happen.

Randy taught history at the university level for three years, until it became obvious that he would not receive tenure. He decided to explore entering business. Randy knew he had very good research and writing skills, but was uncertain as to where to apply them. He also knew that current events held a great interest for him. He was constantly reading.

He began to identify his career direction through extensive reading. Knowing that research and writing skills were his most marketable commodity he began investigating the general field of public relations. He decided public affairs or government relations was the most interesting aspect of this broad field. As a result of his research he became aware of the Public Affairs Council in Washington, D.C. With the aid of the Encyclopedia of Associations, he found the name of the council director and wrote the following letter:

1195 Wisconsin Avenue, N.W.
Washington, D.C. 20007
December 12, 1979

Mr. J. Smith
Director of Public Affairs Council
1220 Roth Street, N.W.
Washington, D.C. 20036

Dear Mr. Smith:

After three years as a professor of European history, I am making a shift to a career in corporate public affairs. I have published several studies that required the integrated investigation of economic, social, and psychological factors, and it is my strong belief that the skills I have developed could be very useful in the analysis of political and social trends affecting the operations of multinational corporations.

I am doing extensive overview research on the emerging needs and issues in the field by reading all the suitable literature and speaking to a wide group of professionals. As part of this research, I would greatly appreciate having a few minutes of your time to share my findings as well as get your professional opinions regarding this field.

Let me make it clear that I am not requesting this meeting to seek a position. What I need is informed and intelligent advice from active professionals like yourself. I will call you next week to see if we can find a time when it would be convenient to meet.

Sincerely,

Randy Peters

At the same time he wrote similar letters to the directors of public affairs in four of the Fortune 100 companies. After the phone calls, Randy managed to arrange three meetings: one with the Executive Director of the PAC and two with directors of public affairs in oil companies. The remaining two directors declined to see Randy. One spoke to him on the phone saying they were not hiring at this time and the other sent his letter to personnel. It's important for the job seeker to note that even though Randy stated he was not asking for a job, two of the five men did not understand the substance of the letter.

Within the next two weeks Randy arranged three meetings. The meeting with the director of the Council was very positive and led to the suggestion to contact a leading consultant in the field who was based in New York. The meetings with the two directors of public affairs were strikingly different. One resulted in a great deal of information for Randy about the company's programs, but no suggestions for future contacts. The other meeting was a "disaster." It lasted only twenty minutes, largely spent criticizing Randy's proposed résumé.

Randy had learned: don't ask advice on résumé writing or on job search. If your agenda is information, keep to it. Randy proceeded by sending letters to four more directors of public affairs of major companies. The letters were similar to those he had previously sent. He also sent a similar letter with the following insert to the consultant who had been recommended: "A mutual colleague of ours, Mr. J. Smith, Director of the Public Affairs Council, suggested I contact you." Randy was beginning to develop a reference system, one of the by-products of creative networking.

From these five letters, four interviews were scheduled: three were with company directors, and one was with the consultant. Two company directors were very helpful in sharing a great deal of information as well as each recommending another person to contact. The third company director referred Randy to a staff assistant; this meeting was not productive. However, the consultant turned out to be a wealth of information. He alerted Randy to the fact that two companies, a major bank and an energy company, were each looking for assistant directors of Public Affairs and that a major chemical company was creating four new positions.

Randy wrote letters to the five referrals that resulted from this round in his networking process. All of this activity had taken about two months. The "map" below illustrates his networking results.

Randy sends five letters.

Letter Results

1. Meeting, Director of the Public Affairs Council
2. Meeting, Director at Company A
3. Meeting, Director at Company B
4. Letter sent to personnel at Company C
5. Phone conversation: "We are not hiring" at Company D

Meeting Results

1. Information and reference to Consultant
2. Information
3. Negative (résumé critique)

Randy sends five more letters.

Letter Results

1. Meeting with referred Consultant
2. Meeting, Director at Company E
3. Meeting, Director at Company F
4. Meeting, Director at Company G
5. No contact after repeated phone calls to Director at Company H

Meeting Results

1. Two references to positions being filled and a reference to a chemical company adding four new positions
2. Information and reference
3. Information and reference
4. Sent to assistant

Randy continued by sending three letters to the people who had been referred to him. He also telephoned the companies the consultant had said were looking for assistant directors. The results of his letters and calls are outlined below:

Randy sends three more letters and calls two companies.

Letter Results

1. Meeting with Director at chemical company
2. Meeting with Director at Company I
3. Phone conversation with Director at Company J—too busy

Phone Results

1. Interviewed three times at bank
2. Interviewed at dinner once with the energy company

Final result—received neither job.

Meeting Results

1. Established good relationship and was told he would be contacted if the board approved the new positions.
2. A referral to another contact.

The networking process had now taken Randy about three months. He had learned a great deal and was becoming visible to many people within the public affairs field. As he continued his networking process, he became more specific about how he could contribute, and he gathered more and more information. He continued this process for another month; meeting more and more people, and thus becoming more informed and visible. He was beginning to feel like a public affairs expert.

After four months of networking, Randy was called by the Director of P.A. from the chemical company whom he had previously met. The board had approved two of the four requested positions and Randy was being considered. After three interviews Randy was hired. This example clearly depicts a creative networking process. The network, as a matrix for the exchange of ideas, worked for Randy, and at the same time provided a means of visibility.

The personal network that you as a job-seeker construct must be of your own design. Once begun, it will require care and maintenance. Review it from time to time, draw schematic maps of it, construct new routes, etc. Do not be reluctant to recontact earlier members—you will have become more valuable to them because of your experiences and network activity and they, in turn, may have new information for you.

THE PROPOSAL

As you become more informed about the current needs within your field, you are frequently in a position to develop proposals. The proposal is a basic element in selling yourself and, accordingly, it should clearly outline what actions are required by the company you are approaching, who should carry out the proposed programs, and what the expected benefits for the company will be. The benefits are crucial. They will attract the interest of the person you are contacting.

If you are just getting started in your career, a proposal may be difficult to make. Remember that business executives are generally interested in something that will help them improve their business. Let's look at some examples.

Lottie was returning to the job market after years of raising her family. She had spent a great deal of time in volunteer work for a variety of organizations in her community, which she used in formulating a proposal. Lottie was interested in the public relations field, and she knew the local banks were concerned about their community relations.

Lorraine was interested in leaving teaching. Her initial proposal started her network in the publishing field and led ultimately to a position in publishing.

246 Rendezvous Drive
Cincinnati, Ohio 45236
November 28, 1979

Mr. Herbert Wise
Director, Community Relations
Fifth Bank
Cincinnati, Ohio 45247

Dear Mr. Wise:

For the past twenty years I have been active in our community, especially in doing public-relations work for a number of nonprofit organizations. In doing this work, I concentrated on community development techniques for organizing local neighborhoods to get grass-roots support for projects. These techniques are directly applicable to community relations for any business, but especially a service business.

The many local branches of the Fifth Bank could significantly improve their community relations through a more active approach to neighborhoods. I am looking for a career opportunity in community relations and would like to meet with you to discuss my ideas.

I will call your office in a week to arrange an appointment.

Sincerely,

Lottie Wrench

686 Beach Avenue
Stamford, Connecticut 06840
November 4, 1980

President
Xerox Publication Division
1 Pickwich Plaza
Greenwich, Connecticut 06830

Dear Mr. Senter:

Feature Films on 8mm and 16mm, edited by James L. Limbacker and published by R. R. Bowker Company, a Xerox Education Company, is an excellent compilation of feature films.

To make an already excellent publication an exceptional one, several alterations in listing films and one additional listing might be considered:

1. A listing of films by theme would help research, especially for teachers of literature who might wish to plan a thematic unit using film.
2. A listing of films by subject (science fiction, adventure, biography) would add another dimension to the publication's use, since literature teachers often plan units of study by such subject matter.

3. The additional listing, I believe, to be most essential. This would be a listing of available study guides developed to assist in using films as instructional media.

As a teacher, it is often impossible to preview every film I use with my classes and, time-wise, completely impossible for me to prepare and write comprehensive and developmental study guides to assist my students in a more total appreciation and understanding of the film.

Often films are used as entertaining rewards after students have read, studied, and discussed the literary work upon which the film is based. Why can't films themselves be the instructional media? Study guides accompanying films would open literary horizons for poorly motivated, reluctant readers. In addition, gifted students might be expected, after guided study of the film, to be led into a comparison-contrast study of the film and its original literary source.

I would welcome an opportunity to discuss with you personally how study guides created to accompany feature films could increase use of *Feature Films on 8mm and 16mm* and, thereby, increase the listed films' rental and sales.

I will call you after you receive this letter to set up an appointment.

Sincerely,

Lorraine W. Kravat

Dominic's objective was to become involved in television. His proposal letter follows:

ABC Company
695 Fifth Avenue
New York, New York 10022

Dear Mr. Jones:

During the past eight years, I have been deeply involved with media education. My experiences range from teaching children to produce television to conducting graduate courses for educators in television utilization and production. In 1976 I was a guest panel speaker at Action for Children's Television's sixth national symposium. During that time, and since, I have developed a broad understanding of network television's need to respond to pressure from such citizen's groups in ways that improve the image of the industry.

I have personally developed many ideas that make television viewing compatible with the ever-increasing demands of both educators and parents. An outstanding example of how television can gain a more respectable image is evident in the Philadelphia TV/Reading Program, which has gained very favorable acclaim with that local market and within the educational community at large.

> This, of course, is just one isolated program that unites the interests of network television with the interests of a more educated and selective public. In my graduate courses, I have developed and outlined many ideas that encourage teachers and parents to utilize the offerings of television; ideas and activities that make young people's viewing experiences more meaningful. In contrast to the advocates of Marie Wynn's "unplug the set" solution, my ideas center around more valuable television utilization within the family structure.
>
> I believe it should be a project of the networks themselves, rather than current federal project proposals, to take the initiative in educating teachers and the general public about the beneficial uses of television. What the federal proposals are currently attempting to do, I have been successfully doing for several years. I have the experience and the know-how to be of great value to your organization in initiating educational and public relations endeavors. I would like to discuss a specific proposal I have in mind with you. I will phone you within the next week in order to arrange a convenient appointment.
>
> Sincerely,
>
> Dominic Prospect

In Dominic's case, his precise proposal was adopted, thus creating a new position for himself.

What all these proposals have in common is that they address themselves to current needs within specific industries. They are wrestling with industry-related problems or ways of developing new markets. A proposal immediately distinguishes its author from the mere job seeker and generally leads to an interview with a professional in the field. Such meetings are not job interviews; they are introductory interviews that begin to establish a new person within the network. Ultimately, they will give personal visibility and access to the employment system.

Once your goal of employment is achieved, you will have no doubt about the effectiveness of operating within a network of people who share some aspects of your aspirations. At this point the network has, in a sense, only begun to work for you. You have created it, benefited from it and now are in a position to extend it, to reach for new goals, and to spend additional time on its maintenance and growth.

Successful career-minded individuals invest a great deal of energy in developing and nourishing their personal networks. Advancement in any field is far from accidental. It is also more than inherent talent; many shining lights remain forever hidden under baskets. To become visible as talented demands continual networking. The *Appendix* presents the recorded experience of a successful networking effort. Study the appendix carefully and you will learn a great deal about the actual process. The notes are based on an actual experience. The names of the executives have, of course, been changed.

In the active phase of networking there are a variety of interviews you can set up, from purely information gathering to proposal meetings. When you begin, you may only be capable of information interviews. The example of Randy in the previous section shows how information interviews can lead to the development of a broad network and ultimate employment.

One difficulty in obtaining information interviews today is that people have misused such settings in the past. Under the guise of seeking information, they have set up interviews and proceeded to ask for a job. Many employers were burnt by such manipulations, and are now skeptical about the authenticity of information seekers.

Proposal interviews, of course, are easier to obtain since there is a greater obvious reciprocity in such a meeting. When your proposal ideas may help the interviewer, it is obviously worth his time to see you.

The proposal interview also has a great value for you, especially if you are changing fields or beginning your career. What it does is enable you to exhibit your knowledge, capabilities, and enthusiasms during a meeting where you are discussing with another professional issues of common concern. Your lack of previous experience within this field, the major obstacle to career change, becomes secondary. You can show through the substance of your proposal that you have already made the transition sufficient to begin work in the new field. Successful interviews of this kind lead to referrals to actual openings that occur. At times positions are created to house new-found talent.

Telephone Follow-Up

In networking, after an initial contact has been made by letter, you should follow up with a telephone call approximately one week later. You will note that the sample letters previously cited end with the promise of a phone call. The objective of this call is to establish a time for a personal meeting. Do not transact your business over the phone.

Since a secretary will usually screen your calls, it is very important to establish an honest, cordial relationship with this person. The following procedures should be followed.

1. State your name and the nature of your business, making sure that your letter was received.

2. If your contact person is busy (He's in a meeting, on the phone, or out for the day), ask the secretary for a more appropriate time to call.

Do not leave your number or ask for your call to be returned since you will then be forced to wait passively.

3. Keep calling, always being pleasant and patient. If by the fifth call (over the period of a week) you are still not able to connect, turn to the secretary. Ask if *she* could check as to whether a personal meeting is possible since it is not your intent to be a nuisance. If you have established a relationship with this person, you at this point have a powerful ally who can facilitate the meeting you want.

If setting up personal meetings demands five—even ten—phone calls, it is important not to assume that your prospective contact has decided not to see you. Wait until you are directly turned down. Many people give up after the fourth call assuming that they have failed. Others, who persist, discover that the fifth call leads to an interview.

THE DYNAMICS OF INTERVIEWING

The successful networker is an expert in building relationships, which is both a skill and an art. Like any skill it is instinctive. A good tennis player, for example, does not self-consciously think how he grips the racket. The racket becomes an extension of his arm and the grip "instinctive." The same is true for people skilled at interpersonal relations. They are characterized by spontaneous warmth, empathy, and genuineness. The successful networker must learn these skills.

In classical job interviews the utilization of relationship skills is frequently extremely difficult, due essentially to the nature of the interview situation. In Figure 25 we describe the interpersonal dynamics of

FIGURE 25 Classical Interview.

INTERVIEWER (Employer)	INTERVIEWER (Job Seeker)
Role — judge-evaluator	— Defandant
Objectives — discern appropriateness and compatibility	— to sell self
Skills — assessment	— Salesmanship
Psychological Posture — Analytic/Guarded	— Defensive/Guarded

Employer (Professional)	Employee (New Professional)
Role: – mentor-colleague	–Advice-colleague
Objectives: – advice-sharing	–to learn and share
Skills: – relationship/counseling	–relationship
Psychological Posture: – Questioning, curious/open	–open/giving

FIGURE 26 Networking Encounter.

the classic job interview by defining the role and objectives of each player, skills being utilized, and psychological postures.

Compare this with an interview between two individuals similar to what happens in effective networking situations. Figure 26 explains the dynamics.

The dynamics of the two situations are 180° apart. In the networking interview, relationship skills are important and can be utilized. This is much less true of classical job interviews, since the dynamics run counter to these skills. They create a guarded, defensive, and self-conscious posture, which no one enjoys.

To counter these dynamics, interviewers are trained to "break the ice" and create an easy atmosphere. It's extremely interesting to note that it is during "ice-breaking" (usually the first five minutes of the interview) that many decisions to hire are made at a subliminal level. Such decisions frequently have little to do with background or job compatibility, and therefore companies are doing more training on interviewing to ensure proper judgments are made. The irony remains; despite extensive training efforts, hiring decisions are still largely based on relationship "vibrations."

Within the classic job interview, the would-be employee is advised to control the situation and sell himself. Such advice is well-intentioned, since it attempts to empower the job seeker, who is being placed in a potentially oppressive situation, with some sense of control. Most self-help books on interviewing fall short however, because they fail to acknowledge the power and importance of the interview structure.

In networking, relationships are established well before an actual job interview occurs. With prior relationships established, the structure of the job interview is radically modified and the utilization of relationship skills becomes possible.

Increasing Your Relationship Skills

Since effective networking rests on relationship skills, it is important to increase your effectiveness in this area as much as possible. There are disagreements among "experts" as to just how much you can change in this area, and yet all would concede that some growth is possible.

While techniques may be learned, increased interpersonal effectiveness arises more from a person's integrated acceptance of himself. We communicate effectively with others to the degree we communicate with the whole of ourselves. By beginning to open up to the neglected side of ourselves, we expand our communication effectiveness to a wider range of people. Assuming you have begun to think with circles about yourself and your career, there are some guides to increasing your relationship skills.

About fifteen years ago a group of psychologists from the humanistic school or Third Force (founded by people like Abraham Maslow, Carl Rogers, and Fritz Perls) did some interesting studies on effective relationships. From their studies they developed a model based on what are called *Core Conditions.* Simply put, the model states that in effective relationships four conditions are communicated at high levels: Empathy, Respect, Genuineness, and Concreteness.

Empathy exists where the listener strives to respond to the speaker's deeper feelings. This is something you can consciously attend to and therefore increase the levels of empathy within communication situations. Concreteness, which involves the fluent and direct expression of your concerns, is another condition which can be controlled. Respect and Genuineness are more difficult to alter, since they are intimately connected to our personality. Since the four conditions are interrelated, by increasing the level of any one, we increase our ultimate effectiveness. Since Empathy and Concreteness as conditions are more controllable, we emphasize these.

An example will help illustrate how empathy increases effectiveness. Assume for a moment that you are a consultant attempting to be hired by a large company to do a series of training programs for their management. What you know going into the interview is that the company has established a new program on career development for their employees. It has been mandated that all managers have to be trained on how to "counsel subordinates regarding their career development in the company." You are being interviewed by the Director of Training within one of the divisions of the company, since he is responsible for executing the company training mandate for his division. Assume also that going into the interview you want the job and have no previous experience with this Director.

The interview begins after ice-breaking with this question: "Do you *really* think *managers* can be trained to do *career counseling*?" In the tonality of the question, the emphasis is placed on the italicized words. Read the question again and respond before proceeding.

Now reflect for a moment on how you responded. Were you selling yourself or the training or were you developing a relationship with the Director by emphasizing empathy? Figure 27 contrasts the behavioral differences between a selling and empathic (high relationship) mode. You will note that the relationship mode takes into consideration more than the simple words of the Director's question. Through keen listening it is obvious that the Director is apprehensive and concerned about the nature of the mandated program. The relationship mode responds to this concern *before* trying to alleviate it. The selling mode tries to dispel the concern without acknowledging its existence.

The relationship mode emphasizing empathy first responds to expressed concerns and then presents possible solutions to the intelligent and legitimate concerns of the Director. In this example, the relationship mode is much more effective in bringing about a consulting contract than the selling mode. The same principle holds for obtaining employment.

FIGURE 27 Two Modes of Response in Interviews.

Selling Mode Examples	Relationship Mode
1) Absolutely, we have had great success in training . . . (Hard sell/Expert) 2) Definitely it's possible. There are some studies at Z company. (Hard sell/Teacher) 3) I think there are some programs that are effective. (Soft sell)	1) It's a good question, because there are some subtle problems in such training. We ask managers to be task oriented and get the job done, we ask them to be evaluators of employees and now we're asking them to play a role of counselor. The counselor-evaluator roles are very opposite, etc. On the other hand, since its a mandated program, there are some training designs which can be effective, etc. (Empathic/Expert)

FROM NETWORKING TO JOB INTERVIEWING

Eventually the networking process leads to referrals and job interviews. The fact that you are referred results in more trust and openness from the beginning, therefore relationship skills are more important. If you have successfully reframed your approach, this will also modify the nature of the interview. You will be hiring the employer as much as he is hiring you.

Frequently, job searchers look for months for precisely the right opportunity. Eventually they find and take a position and yet feel they must honor interviews which they scheduled prior to accepting their new job. These interviews go well and they are offered jobs in several cases. This experience can be seen as pure chance or as a result of the interviewee *not seeking* (begging for) a position. Because he has already accepted a new job, his posture is fully reframed and consequently he starts being pursued.

In order to successfully reframe as we describe it here, you must be free from economic pressures which force you into begging postures. Therefore if you are: (1) changing careers, you should stay employed while networking to make the transition; (2) entering work from college, you should begin networking at least six months before graduating; (3) a woman seeking to reenter work, allow yourself six months to network before you expect to begin; (4) unemployed, it may be wise to take temporary work while you network for your desired objective.

In summary, to maximize job search effectiveness two fundamental reframing processes are necessary—your understanding of how the employment system works and your attitude toward your own employment. When these changes occur, you are capable of networking. This process informs you of current needs within specific fields, gives you access to the majority of employment opportunities, and makes you visible to those who do the hiring.

Being Interviewed

When the networking process leads to actual job interviews, you should be prepared for what may happen. Since conducting these interviews is frequently as discomforting for managers as for job searchers, it will add to your success if you can help to make the meeting relaxed and enjoyable. Being prepared helps you to create this atmosphere. Part of being prepared is being properly dressed. Don't be overdressed and don't be too informal or you will distract from the interview. Common, good manners are also important—shaking hands, speaking clearly, etc.

No interview is the same, but there are some common questions which you should be prepared to answer. In Figure 28, Column A lists five questions commonly asked in job interviews. In Column B are five questions you should be prepared to explore if the interview becomes an exercise in testing you. This sometimes happens at higher level positions or for positions sought by people in mid-career changes.

COLUMN A	COLUMN B
1. Tell me a little about yourself?	1. What is your philosophy of management?
2. What are your strengths?	2. How would you contribute to our organization?
3. What are your limitations?	3. What are your reservations regarding the position?
4. What are your major accomplishments?	4. Why are you leaving your current position?
5. What are your aspirations? 5, 10 years from now?	5. What in this position will be most difficult for you?

FIGURE 28 Common Interviewing Questions.

Be specific and direct in your response. Your answers should be present and future oriented as opposed to lengthy and biographic. For example, to the question tell me a little about yourself, a concrete articulation of your *present* objective is much more effective than narratives about your past. Résumés are designed to cover the past. The best preparation for any interview is having a solid grasp of the current needs and trends in the function and industry you are approaching. The major intent of the series which this book introduces is to guide you to this kind of information. Successful networking will also produce this kind of understanding.

The Other Side of the Desk

Most managers are not highly skilled in interviewing. As a result, many spend most of the time talking themselves instead of listening. If this occurs, help the situation by listening empathically and directing the conversation toward a dialogue. By knowing what a good interviewer should do, you are able to help him with his task. Essentially, this is to determine whether you are appropriate for the position. It's to your advantage to do this, since accepting the incorrect position is detrimental to your ultimate career development.

Generally, interviewers are taught to assess a candidate's intelligence, personality, experience, and motivation as these relate to job requirements. A good interviewer will structure the meeting and ask the kind of questions which will enable him to assess these four qualities. To do this he will ask broad-brush or open-ended questions which do not permit a simple yes or no answer. These questions will usually begin with a "what," "how," or "why" and permit you great latitude in your response. Be concrete and genuine in answering.

Figure 29 shows a typical model for interviewing that is taught to managers.

1. Create relaxed atmosphere
2. Structure the session
3. School experience
4. Early Work
5. Recent responsibilities
6. Self-assessment
7. Career Opportunities
8. Job Requirements
9. Test questions
10. Outside Interests
11. Summary
12. Closing

FIGURE 29 An Outline for Structuring Interviews. Adapted from "How to Conduct Interviews," *Executive Skills,* November 1978 (New York: AMACOM, a Division of American Management Associations, 1978), p. 8.

NETWORKING AS AN ENTRY-LEVEL CANDIDATE

It is possible to create a network for yourself during your college years that leads directly to employment. Consider the case of Melinda who was studying as an undergraduate in the field of gerontology. Between her freshman and sophomore years, she worked as a research assistant on a federally funded project examining services for the elderly. She got the position by following a tip from one of her professors. A letter to the project director did the trick. By doing a good job that summer, she was able to continue doing research for the project and at the same time get course credit through independent research courses available in her department. Throughout the year, she made it a point to meet every professional in gerontology who was in the area surrounding her college. She used the research project involvement as a way of networking this group, sharing project information in return for information on what professionals were involved in.

Through this activity, she was offered three different summer jobs, but chose to return to the research project. She was able to develop a solid relationship with the project director, which led to more contacts with top-level people in the profession and an offer to assist the director in doing research for a new book. By the time her senior year came, Melinda had three possible positions to take and was able to make a real choice. Her network of contacts was solidly established and she had access to the most recent information in the gerontological field. She was even involved, before graduating, in projects that were creating new information.

You see from Melinda's activity how it is possible and even desirable to begin networking during college study. Too many make the mistake of doing nothing until the last minute and then start the job hunt cold after graduation.

ON RESUMES

Résumés are a means of making yourself visible as a valuable asset to a prospective employer. In this sense it is a selling vehicle, a means of attracting attention. We have noted earlier in this chapter the limitations of sending résumés as a means of job search. Despite these limitations, it remains important to have a document which persuasively presents your capabilities and aspirations. Even in networking, where you usually do not use a résumé, have a good one available to leave if your contact person asks for it. No effective résumé can be prepared if you have no job objective. It would be like an advertiser preparing an ad without understanding his product or market. Résumés should begin with *very specific* career objectives. If you are interested in three or four objectives and cannot focus more precisely, then create three or four résumés, one for each objective.

Here are two examples of specific objectives.

1. A position as a sales representative for a company in the solar energy field.
2. A position in training and development within the insurance industry, with special emphasis on career development programs.

After stating your objective, follow with a brief summary paragraph highlighting your skills and accomplishments which show that your objective is realistic in terms of what you are capable of contributing. This paragraph should summarize the entire résumé.

Functional and Chronological Résumés

There are basically two formats you can follow in preparing your résumé—functional or chronological. For people without extensive experience or who are changing careers, the functional format is preferable. Two examples of well-written functional résumés are given here. You will note that they contain a brief historical section which most employers want to see.

You notice that all formats include other sections such as education, organizational membership, and personal information. The personal section is purely a matter of preference, not essential. Whatever format you choose, make sure that the final product is:

1. Graphically attractive—well typed, good margins, and generally professional in appearance.
2. Proper length—usually no more than two pages.
3. Concrete—skills and accomplishments are stated in very specific terms, not generalities. Give numbers, percentages, products, etc.
4. Well written—no spelling or grammatical mistakes, dominated by action-oriented statements, preferably in sentences of no more than ten words.

DAVID SASSOON
4 Albino Way
San Francisco, California 94101

(415) 555–3742

Objective: A position as a management trainee in the banking industry.

SUMMARY

I am completing my degree in economics in which I specialized in the banking field. I have worked for three consecutive summers as a teller in our neighborhood bank, becoming familiar with day-to-day operations. I have a special interest in the application of information systems to banking procedures and have recently learned to operate a microcomputer.

WORK EXPERIENCE

Summers, 1977, 1978, 1979	Teller, Branch Office, Bank of California
1974 - 1976 (part time)	Assistant Manager, Safeway Stores

EDUCATION

B.A. Economics University of California, Berkeley

PERSONAL

Hobbies: Home-information systems, jogging, tennis, travel.

DENISE M. WRIGHT
14 West Dorchester Road
Houston, Texas 77002

(713) 555–8746

Objective: A position as a human-relations specialist with an organization working with industry, business, community, and educational institutions.

SUMMARY

I have thirteen years of diversified experience creating and implementing programs, writing press releases, speaking in public, and raising funds for a variety of organizations. Working for the benefit of different groups and becoming sensitive to their individual needs has been central to my career.

QUALIFICATIONS

Consultant to the Women's Center for Career Planning, Union County, New Jersey. I assist in meeting the needs and interests of contemporary women who are aware that lifestyles are changing and who want information and support to meet new life expectations.

Career Counselor, Union County Technical Institute and Vocational Center, New Jersey. I have administered aptitude tests, assisted in the exploration of career and nontraditional career information, employment seeking and mid-life career change information. I have worked with clients on a one-to-one basis and also in group settings to assist in the area of expansion of self-awareness, career awareness, and identification of relevant career alternatives. I have been a facilitator in the areas of exploration, evaluation, and assessment of various career options.

Group Leader and Facilitator in programs associated with the Archdiocese of Newark, New Jersey. Group process and group dynamics form an integral part of these experiential programs . . . Marriage Encounter, Days of Recollection, and the Crossroads and Search Programs for young adults. As part of these programs, I assist the participants in the opportunity of becoming more aware of themselves as persons and more aware of their human potential by providing the climate in which they can explore the meaning of their own lives, their relationships with family and friends, what they have to offer, how they can grow, their freedom to choose between alternatives, and a sense of responsibility for their own growth.

Director and Coordinator of Service Program at a private school, New Jersey. Supervision of 180 students, involving group members in program planning, selection of activities most appropriate for the age, experience, and background of the student.

Graduate Assistant, Office of Student Affairs, Kean College of New Jersey. I was responsible for planning and coordinating social, recreational, and educational enrichment programs for the student body. As a member of the Dean of Students staff, I was advisor to the International Students Association and was Assistant to the Director of the Student Aide Program. Also responsible for selection, acquisition, and presentation of a weekly film program.

Director of Summer Vacation School Program. I organized, planned, and developed the program; was responsible for curriculum selection, recruitment of teachers and youth assistants.

COMMUNITY AND PUBLIC RELATIONS

—Elected District Committeewoman.
—Elected Trustee of Scotch Plains-Fanwood Scholarship Foundation, Inc.
—Elected Secretary of College Women's Club of Scotch Plains-Fanwood.
—Elected member of Parish Advisory Board and Archdiocesan Pastoral Council.
—Coordinator of Girl Scout Troup.
—Executive Board Member of P.T.A.
—President of Church Women's Society where enrollment increased from 85 to 210 members during my two-year term of office.
—Member of Two Worlds Service Committee . . . assisted in the formation of a Group Foster Home, Renaissance House, in Plainfield, New Jersey.

EDUCATION

M.A. 1976	Kean College of New Jersey.
B.S. 1958	Fordham University, New York, Major: Education Minor: Speech and Public Speaking.
1976–1977	Georgetown University, School of Summer Program for Continuing Education.

MEMBERSHIPS

Kappa Delta Pi Honor Society
American Personnel and Guidance Association

References furnished upon request

The chronological résumé is the most frequently used format. It is the easiest to prepare since names and dates are more readily described than skills. It is also more familiar to employers. Here are two examples.

CAROLINE MEAGERS
4209 Evans Place
Waterbury, Connecticut 06701

(203) 555–7023

Objective: Assistant-editorial responsibility in a publishing company.

EXPERIENCE

Summer 1979 Research Assistant, Mainstream Access, New York, New York. Researched various fields and organized material for clients seeking a career change. Wrote résumés. Did some editorial work on guides to the major fields in business. Discussed program on the phone with prospective clients, and assisted the office manager: used a word processor (videotype 91) and handled filing and correspondence.

Senior Year Associate Editor, Jonathan Edwards Literary Magazine. Reestablished defunct magazine, launched campaign to solicit submissions, determined format and layout with associates. Drank a lot of coffee.

Master's Aide, Jonathan Edwards College, Yale University. Responsible for development of a new college program: the Jonathan Edwards Forum, including publicity, assessing student interest, and invitations. Assisted with all aspects of the college's routine.

Jonathan Edwards College Printer, Jonathan Edwards College, Yale University. Designed and produced (on hand presses): posters, invitations, and menus.

Assistant Guitar Teacher, Yale Student Tech Agency, Yale University. Weekly lessons to a group of twelve.

Summer 1978 Codirector, First Annual Community Return Fundraising Art Exhibit, (the sidewalks of) Stamford, Connecticut. Helped organize the exhibit, wrote press releases, solicited corporate contributions by letter and phone, contacted local artists, and arranged for their participation.

Assistant Pretrial Coordinator; publicity agent, Community Return, Stamford Superior Courthouse, Stamford, Connecticut. Interviewed overnight prisoners and determined their roots in the community. Petitioned the court for a lower bail when deemed appropriate. Followed up each prisoner's progress in court. Reorganized files and developed publicity and fundraising systems.

Summer 1977 Part-time secretary, Brad Hvolbeck Realtors, Greenwich, Connecticut. Assistant household management, Charlotte and William O'Shea, Greenwich, Connecticut (family of seven).

EDUCATION

B.A. Yale University

PETER R. CROWN
1841 West 3rd Avenue
New York, New York 10001
(212) 555–0202

Objective: A management or marketing position as a communications specialist.

CAREER SUMMARY:

Experience in the field of COMMUNICATIONS with major emphasis on employee benefits, CONSULTING, WRITING, rewriting, EDITING, and LANGUAGE SIMPLIFICATION of technical material into plain English.

BUSINESS EXPERIENCE:

July 1977–present

Communications Consultant (7/77–3/78) and Manager, Communications Department (3/78–10/78) Martin Smith Co., New York, New York

Responsibility centered on the writing, rewriting, editing, and production of all communications products of the major Employee Benefits Actuarial Consulting Firm. The department, serving both corporate and multiemployer clients, billed more than $1,000,000 in 1977–78.

As a *Communications Consultant,* I was involved in developing plain English prototypes for communications products—summary plan descriptions (pension, profit-sharing, and group insurance plans), summary annual reports, benefits statements, public relations brochures, slide presentations, surveys. I worked with account executives, plan administrators, insurance carriers, personnel executives and actuaries I also coordinate outside freelance writers and vendors.

As *Department Manager,* I was involved in supervising the work of four writers, an administrative assistant, and a production assistant. Managing caseload assignments, scheduling, and deadlines. Reviewing materials, negotiating fees, recruiting and training writers in techniques of language simplification and readability analysis. Internal marketing, research, and seminars.

My achievements include the preparation of a major government proposal (bid: $82,000) submitted to the Department of Labor.

PETER R. CROWN
page 2

March June 1977	Staff Writer, Medical Economics Magazine, Oradell, New Jersey. Wrote feature articles and shorts on financial topics for this prestigious business magazine for doctors.
July 1976 March 1977	Freelance Editor/Writer/Rewriter for American Book Co., Holt Rinehart & Winston, Harcourt Brace Javanovich, Inc., Equitable Life Assurance Society, New York, New York Projects included writing to specific grade levels for elementary reading and mathematics series, readability analysis, and rewriting a consumer-oriented insurance booklet in plain English.
EDUCATION;	AB, English, Providence College, Providence, Rhode Island, 1976.
PROFESSIONAL MEMBERSHIP:	Publicity Club of New York
PERSONAL:	Age: 25 Health: Excellent Languages: Fluency in Italian and French.
REFERENCES:	Upon Request.

Of course there is also a format which combines the chronological and functional. James's résumé below is an example.

JAMES HILLMAN
742 Meadowbrook
Corpus Christi, Texas 78412

(512) 555–8282

Career Objective: Responsibility for the selling of advertising in TV, radio and/or publications.

SUMMARY

I have been in the creative sales field for the past seven years. My strength is in creating new markets as well as expanding existing ones by my ability to communicate and create confidence in the customer. My experience is diverse, involving service organizations and also products. I have also been involved in management, led seminar groups, marketed and planned distribution for a new product.

QUALIFICATIONS

As a *Sales Representative* with American Silk Mills, I created a new market in silk-blended fabrics for the volume Sportswear market. I increased company profits by 200% in this product line. I was also able to maintain customer loyalty in the highly competitive fashion industry.

As a *Marketing* and *Promotional* person, I worked on a campaign of introduction for a new perfume product line. I designed the entire marketing plan and implemented it through personally supervised sales work.

As a *Banker,* I was involved in retail banking and creating new customers for expanding retail banking services.

As an *Administrator,* I managed a Holiday Inn and was involved in all aspects of innkeeping, providing me with a good, practical education in dealing with the public.

JAMES HILLMAN
page 2

EXPERIENCE

1978–Present	Sales and Marketing Representative for Designer Perfumes, Inc., Groton, Connecticut
1975–1978	Sales Representative, American Silk Mills, New York City, New York
1972–1974	Sales Representative, Spring Mills, New York City, New York
1971–1972	Retail Banking Counselor, Manufacturers Hanover Trust Company, New York City, New York
1968–1971	Assistant Innkeeper and Sales Representative, Holiday Inn Motel, Groton, Connecticut

EDUCATION

B.A., University of Tampa, Tampa Florida

References Available on Request

SUMMARY

As you see from this detailed description, networking takes time and hard work. If you need a job immediately, take it and then begin to organize your network. It is necessary if you want to take control of your career and design it yourself. Once you learn the skills of networking, you will have them for the rest of your life. Not only that, you have control over the future of your career, something only a few people possess.

Many people start a networking process and then back out when they realize how much time and hard work is involved. Unfortunately, they will probably never experience the rewards of a job truly suited to their interests and skills; nor will they have a sense of control over their work, thus restoring its dignity. By creating an effective personal network, you can move successfully through your business career. Yes, it takes time, but if you invest the necessary time, the returns will be great.

A FINAL NOTE

This book began by looking at the central problem of work in today's world—most people no longer own what they produce but are merely means of production. To have meaning and dignity, work must belong to us and be in our control. Career development and career planning must relate directly to this central problem of work in the modern world to have any significance.

As you saw in Chapter 1, the task of taking control of your work requires second-order change and all the struggle which that entails. The struggle involves personal change for you. It also involves change on the part of organizations. We have tried to provide a method based on thinking in terms of the whole—thinking with circles—with which you can relate your own career planning and development to this larger struggle. By so doing you can eliminate the despair that characterizes how too many feel about their work. This is *your work for the eighties* through which you develop yourself as well as the planet.

APPENDIX: A NETWORKING DIARY

This Appendix contains the weekly reports of an especially effective networking process that took place over a six-month period. The networking was for the purpose of a job search and resulted in a number of job offers. The individual responsible for the work, Michael Breslin, was making a major mid-career shift, leaving the Roman Catholic priesthood. His abilities were considerable, and he had been in significant managerial positions as a priest. He saw himself as an effective manager and took a very pragmatic approach to the networking, in that he was open to opportunities in a number of areas. His initial objectives involved international marketing and public relations. As you will see as you study his diary, the network he developed modified his objectives while leading to an exciting management opportunity with a major utility.

Some important lessons can be learned from these notes. The hard work involved will be obvious. So will the ups and downs. The importance of being open to how the process changes you as you engage in it is clearly illustrated here also. Starting the process by contacting associations that are related to your objectives is generally a good idea. It certainly paid off in this instance. At the end of all the work is a network of professionals to whom you are visible and who can be carefully cultivated as a support system in your effort to accomplish your goals.

Michael's résumé, which follows, will give you some background information so that you can better understand his networking. The weekly reports are reproduced here as they were written, except for executive name changes.

MICHAEL BRESLIN
563 Sterling Place
Brooklyn, New York 11238

Work: (212) 555-3166
Residence: (212) 555-1586

Career Objective: Responsibility for domestic and/or international sales programs.

SUMMARY

Fifteen years of professional experience relating to diverse groups of people from varied economic and cultural backgrounds. Exceptional language ability in French and Spanish, including in-depth experience in various countries using these languages. Proven management ability in complex organizational situations with special talent for bringing divergent factions together. Exceptional ability to relate to top managements' concerns with foreign markets. Familiarity with current problems of foreign companies in Quebec. Extensive experience in adult education and training; skilled in interviewing and evaluating personnel.

QUALIFICATIONS

Management: Appointed youngest-ever Pastor, Our Lady of Mercy Church, Brooklyn, New York. 1000 active members, 85% poor Hispanic, 15% poor Black. Full responsibility for professional staff, investment of $700,000 portfolio, maintenance of $1 million facility, and training/utilization of over 100 leaders of special programs. Congregation is one of few financially solvent in area, assumed financial and moral leadership in developing union of 300 local churches, income increased by 50%. Staff methodology used repeatedly as exemplar for other congregations. Area representative to Priests' Senate, one of 35 top advisors to Bishop of Brooklyn. Well-developed ability to manage trouble-shooting responsibility.

Language/Culture: Read, write and fluently speak French and Spanish. Read, write and speak some Creole. Detailed knowledge of cultures related to these languages derived from personal travel and living in specific countries—France, Spain, Belgium, and Paraguay. Extensive travel throughout South America, Mexico, Caribbean and Europe with active network of professional contacts in these areas among community leaders and consumers.

Communications/Sales: Excellent writing and public speaking skills with broad experience in both areas across cultures. The depth of my experience in other cultures combined with my tri-lingual ability makes me a seasoned judge of market realities. I am capable of major responsibility for special projects relating to problems in foreign markets. My leadership ability and ease with all types of people are well established. Specialized training in community organizing techniques has application to market research. Recently published an Adult Education manual in 4 languages and personally supervised its very successful international distribution and sale.

MICHAEL BRESLIN

EXPERIENCE

Pastor/Administrator, Our Lady of Mercy, Brownsville:	1974–present
Area Representative, Priests' Senate: Chairman, Education Committee representing Brownsville, Bushwick, East New York	1975–present
Tri-lingual ministry and chaplain, St. Teresa's, Brooklyn, and Brooklyn Jewish Hospital	1969–1974
Co-Founder, Diocesan Mission Coronel Oviedo, Paraguay	1968–1969
Associate, St. Ephrem's, Brooklyn	1966–1968

EDUCATION

Cathedral College, New York, New York	6 years Classical curriculum
Immaculate Conception Seminary Long Island, New York	B.A. Philosophy Major in English Literature Minor in Public Speaking
University of Louvain, Belgium	4 years, M.A. Theology, S.T.B.
Maryknoll Language Institute—Spanish Cochabamba, Bolivia	
Lake Forest College, Illinois	Specialized Workshop for developing and supervising Adult Training Programs.

PUBLICATIONS

Have written extensively for the *N.Y. Times, The Tablet,* and a national professional newsletter. Published and translated an Adult Education manual.

PROGRESS REPORT FOR MAINSTREAM ACCESS

WEEK OF JULY 10, 1979

Update on associations contacted:

1. American Marketing Association (A.M.A.), 420 Lexington Av. 10017
   appointment to see director, Mr. Paul McDaniel, on July 11, 1979.

2. Sales Executives Club of NY (S.E.C., NY), 112 E. 42 10017
   spoke to Ms. Anne Francis Amato, ass't to director, referred to: Mr. Andrew F. Houlihan, Exec. Dir. and also Director, INTERNATIONAL EXECUTIVES ASS'N.—app't to be made 7/11/79.

3. Sales and Marketing Executives International, 380 Lex. 10017
   spoke to Ms. Barbara Landon, ass't to Exec. V.P., told me to write him and call for app't. week of Aug. 6. Mr. Alfred Milk, Exec. V.P.

4. American Petroleum Institute, 2101 L St. WASH. DC 20037
   spoke to Mr. Herschel Drinkwater, referred to Dr. Robert Bough in "policy analysis"—app.'t to see July 27, 1979.

WEEK OF JULY 17, 1979

July 11	Interview with Mr. Paul McDaniel, director of NY office of American Marketing Ass'n. He has only 1 *week* experience in managing this association, is not familiar with the marketing field nor does he know executives in marketing. He suggests I contact the Advertising Research Foundation, and that I become a member of A.M.A. as an entrée to top executives.
July 13	Interview with Mr. Andrew F. Houlihan, executive director of Sales Executives, Club of NY and director of International Executives Association. In a *2½ hour* interview, we exchanged information on international marketing and techniques of job search. He invited me to a few sessions at the Man Marketing Council, a service of S.E.C. NY. He asked me to conduct a class at Marymount College for Mr. Syms, one of his members. It was agreed that I would return in the near future and that he would then help me make personal contacts.
July 16 & 17	Spoke to Mr. Robert Richards, new directior of National Foreign Trade Council. He showed interest, referred me to: Mr. Donald L'Or—V.P. for Int'l Affairs specializing in Regional Markets, 10 yrs. experience in Venezuela for Westinghouse, set up *July 18 interview,* Mr. Peters to join us if necessary. (*N.B. 2 top oil men* are officers of their board). This Council serves as main information source for Int'l Execs.
July 18	Interview at N.F.T.C.—see next report.
July 18	Interview at Center for Creative Public Service Inc.—jobs for Hispanics, director, John Cordova, a former classmate, who is offering me position as job counselor and help in contacting our colleagues in business fields as well as in education.
July 18	Sent résumé to Mrs. Peggy Polanck, a friend, top exec. in an international cosmetics firm making Oil of Olay, etc. will help me contact Senior V.P.
July 18	Sent résumé to Mr. Arnold Grange, director Syracuse Office of State Mental Health Division. A former colleague who will circulate résumé in Syracuse business community.

WEEK OF JULY 30, 1979

July 18	Interview with Mr. Donald L'Or—V.P. International affairs at the National Foreign Trade Council Lengthy discussion on role of Church in Latin America. Recommended I aim at V.P. International Public Relations in each major corp.—rather than marketing. Listed 18 corps. especially active in Latin America—8 are pharmaceutical. Recommended Council of the Americas as a good grouping of Latin American businesses owned by U.S. firms.
July 18	Interview at Center for Creative Public Service—26 Broadway with director Israel Fein and field director, John Cordova. Was offered a position helping to obtain government-subsidized positions for Hispanics at a straight commission of $200 per person *hired* in addition to a salary of $5,600 for 2 days/wk. of counseling (*no* fringe benefits). Was offered a position as full-time counselor/job finder in Sept. at $14,000 (with fringe benefits). Was offered a position at $20,000 within 1 yr. as field director. Response requested by Aug. 13.
July 27	Interview with Dr. Robert Bough, policy analyst at the American Petroleum Institute, Wash. DC. States that they have no specialist in international affiliates. Long discussion trading policy information. Recommendations to be contacted using *his name:* 1. make direct contact with V.P. Marketing & V.P. Int'l P.R. execs. in New York based corps.: Exxon, Mobil, Continental, Texaco. 2. check out World Petroleum Congress. 3. see Matthew Licht at the Petroleum Industrial Research Center (N.Y.C.) called PIRINC—very well connected in the industry. 4. see P. A. Goldman—at M.I.T.—author of *World Oil Market.* 5. see Dr. William Kott—investment advisor for Salomon Bros. N.Y.C. 6. see Arthur Paul—UCLA Grad. School of Management, wrote *The Multinationals,* knows SOCONY. 7. see Anthony Sampson, author of *The Seven Sisters.* 8. see Albert Donaldson, special assistant for energy to Zbigniew Bryzinski on Nat'l. Security Council: White House. 9. contact Dept. of Energy, Wash. DC—International Shop.

WEEK OF AUG. 6, 1979

Aug. 6	Called Mr. Alfred Milk, Exec. V.P. for Sales & Marketing Executives Intern'l. 122 E. 42 10017 (represents 3,000,000 sales people.) who agreed to see me on Aug. 7.
Aug. 7	1 hour interview with Mr. Milk Very friendly reception when I happened to mention his friend Andrew Houlihan, director of Sales Execs. Club of NY, was impressed by length of interview ("Finn doesn't give 2½ hrs. to his mother.") Very interested in my background and plans, he asked for my résumé & P.A.R.s, and offered to call me with some leads in the near future.
Aug. 9	Located all three major contacts recommended by Dr. Andrew B. Crawford of the American Petroleum Institute: Dr. William Kott—Salomon Brothers for energy. Mr. Robert Candle—director, Petroleum Industry Research Associates Prof. P. A. Goldman—M.I.T. Dept. of Economics Their secretaries advised as to available dates. I will write to them today.

Aug. 9	Called Mr. Jonathan Arlington at the Conference Board *re* the soon-to-be-published study of companies' International Issues and Economists. He told me this study is being edited and will be published by the end of September by a member of his staff, Dr. Stewart Cifer. I have not decided whether to contact him at once or to wait until I have read his study.
Aug. 9	Heard from a friend in international marketing who is presenting my résumé to Mr. Herb Strennan, an active international marketer.
Aug. 9	Began research on the Town of Dennis, MA, after my application for Exec. Secretary of the Board of Selectmen was accepted.

WEEK OF AUG. 13, 1979

Aug. 13	Refused $14,000 offer of employment at the Center for Creative Research.
Aug. 15	Made an appointment to see Mr. Robert Candle, Director of Petroleum Industry Research Associates, recommended by Dr. Bough of A.P.I.
Aug. 15	Made an appointment to see Dr. William Kott of Salomon Bros. recommended by Dr. Bough of A.P.I.
Aug. 15	Called the town of Dennis, MA, to determine how applicants for the position of Exec. Sec. to Board of Selectmen would be notified to come for interview; called Diocese of Fall River to plug into local clergy network; researched the area of Dennis and environs in Nat'l. Catholic Directory and Atlas.
Aug. 17	Received 3 recommendations from a friend at Western Electric, NC. 1. Mr. Rubin of TASA Inter'l, Miami—a *head hunter* for work in foreign cultures.—to use name of Mr. Bill Stevenson of CIBA-GEIGY, Greensboro, NC. 2. Mr. Roger Atterbury, Director Marketing, West. Electric Int'l., Greensboro, NC—for advice and counsel. 3. Try AT&T, 195 B'way—they are *hiring* for foreign assignments.

WEEK OF AUGUST 20, 1979

Aug. 23	Met Mr. Robert Candle, Exec. Director of PIRINC (Petroleum Industry Research Associates) at recommendation of Dr. Bough of A.P.I. He recommended contacting the international headquarters of Mobil, Exxon and Texaco in Coral Gables, FL., as well as Occidental Petroleum in CA—nat. gas & oil in Peru, and Eric Hundman, energy specialist for World Bank—a personal friend. And in the U.N.—Sabastian Tannen—754–8764—Robert Kelly—754–8600—in field of energy resources. And Imperial Oil, Exxon's rep. in Montreal, Ottawa.
Aug. 23	Received a letter from a friend in international cosmetics marketing. She suggests and has spoken to some of the following: 1. Mr. Donald Oliver, V.P. Vick Int'l—Latin America, Far East. Div. of Richardson Merrill (Westport, CT, 8 Wright St.) 2. Mr. Paul McAnty, General Manager, Vick Int'l. 3. Mr. William Peterson, V.P. Personnel Europe/Africa Div.—Vick Int'l., 18 rue Jean Giraudox, Paris. 4. Mr. Ralph Witt, Chairman, Young & Rubicam—285 Madison, NY. 5. Mr. Walter Nadel, Creative Business Mgr., Doyle, Dane, Bernbach—437 Madison, NY. 6. Mr. Darrell Amici, V.P., Philip Morris—100 Park Av.—friend of Shaw.
Aug. 24	Dr. Kott (Salomon Bros.) called to change our appointment to first week in Sept.

WEEK OF AUG. 27, 1979

Aug. 27 — Called Mr. Donald Oliver, Vick Int'l.—will be back Sept. 4.

Called town of Dennis MA—applicants for Exec. Sec'y still not notified.

Called Dr. Stewart Cifer, Conference Bd. author—back on Aug. 29.

Called Mr. Brown and made app't for Aug. 30.

Aug. 29 — Made luncheon app't. with Dr. Williamson for Sept. 4 to discuss int'l issues.

Aug. 30 — Visited Mr. Sabastian Tannen, director of U.N. Dept. of Technical Corporation for Development; Center for Natural Resources, Energy & Transport. Recommended by Mr. Candle of PIRINC.

We discussed theology, Latin America, celibacy, etc.

He was interested in my language ability, how I got to know Brown and my aggressive approach and positive motivation. He recommended:

1. the possibility of a job opening in his department in spring 1980.

2. Greg Stassel (754–3454), director U.N. Center for Transnationals. They establish a code of conduct for transnational corporations and relate to local government.

3. Mr. François Ferdinand (a French Basque), U.N. Personnel Director, in terms of work in the U.N. Dept. of Social Affairs & programs for youth, aged and women in less developed countries. They are losing personnel because they plan to move to Vienna.

Additional recommendations: Mr. Eric Hundman, ass't. director for Energy, World Bank. Recommended by Robert Candle of PIRINC.

Union Carbide (moving to Danbury, CT) recommended by Margaret Swift *and* Center for Creative Public Service.

American Home Products, Mr. Charles Dore, Chairman of the Board, recommended by Dr. L'Or (Nat'l. Foreign Trade Council) *and* Center for Creative Public Service: member: Volunteer Urban Consulting Group, Inc.—getting job careers for minorities (more on this latter available if interested).

Shearson, Hayden, Stone—expanding from Kuhn, Loeb, Inc. to entire 8th fl., World Trade Center.

Mr. Sean O'Connell—Personnel.
Dr. Jerome Schauer—V.P.
Mr. Michael Kean, was Managing Director of Kuhn, Loeb—another member, Volunteer Urban Group.

P.S. Sept. 1 through Thanksgiving—time reserved for job interviews. This will be right on schedule but still mixed with visits to some well-placed association personnel.

WEEK OF SEPT. 1, 1979

July and August '79 — Primary period of visits to ASSOCIATIONS for advice, counsel and orientations:

List of Associations Developed—31

Associations Selected for Visit & Visited—13

Associations Selected but not yet Visited—2

Sept., Oct., Nov. '79 — Primary period of JOB INTERVIEWS:

List of interviews resulting from visits to professional associations—33

Of these, number of primary interest—20

Including contact person—11

WEEK OF SEPT. 3, 1979

Sept. 4 — Phone conversation with Mr. Donald Oliver of Vick Int'l. in Conn. He offered to help me meet Mr. Louis Norton, a resigned priest in charge of their Japan operations, to meet me in NYC next week and to invite me to his home in Westchester.

Sept. 5 — Lunch with Dr. Stewart Cifer, Conference Board author of new book on Int'l Environments and Issues. He feels that corporations show little concern about political, social and regulatory matters and will be unlikely to hire a specialist in this area. Top management prefer to handle this in person. Taking a specialized position puts you in a closed box. Better to go in the front door of major corps. and get right into general management administration or domestic P.R. International operations are usually a backwater and only 150 corps. have major int'l branches. He suggests I emphasize my interest in business and keep my special skills in reserve as a backup. Always get a reading on the corp. and study their end-of-year report before the interview.

He suggested contacting the following:

1. Mr. Jonathan Arlington, Conference Board for advice and counsel on domestic P.R. possibilities.

2. Mr. Ralph Washoe at EXXON NY for career in int'l. public relations.

3. Mr. Leonard Bush at TEXACO NY for career in int'l public relations.

4. Mr. Ronald Blunt at XEROX—in charge of Corporate Affairs—domestic P.R.

Sept. 7 — Interview with Mr. Greg Stassel, director of U.N. Center for Fundamentals. We discussed their "Code of Conduct" for multi-national corps. and how they relate to local gov'ts. He gave me copies of a major study indicating the recent involvement of many medium-sized corps. in foreign countries as well as all developments in finalizing the "Code." He indicated that the quota system for hiring Americans (no more than 25%) left him no openings at the moment but that this could change in a few months.

He suggested:

1. contacting Mr. Litinis, author of the "Code" scheme.

2. U.N. Development Program—personnel dept. They have their own separate personnel office and budget (Dr. Cifer emphasizes that the U.N. pays well but often fires a U.S. employee when a foreign equivalent becomes available).

3. I call him in 1 week for more specific recommendations after he has had time to study my résumé and P.A.R.s.*

WEEK OF SEPT. 10, 1979

Sept. 10 — Wrote personal letters to and requested job interview from:

1. Mr. John O'Malley, V.P. Union Carbide.

Recommended by Dr. L'Or (NFTC), Center for Creative Public Service, & Margaret Swift—moving to Danbury CT.

2. Mr. Ronald Blunt—International P.R. for Xerox, Stamford, CT.

Recommended by Dr. Stewart Cifer, Conference Board.

Sept. 11 — Spoke to Mr. Donald Oliver, Vick Int'l. He put off our meeting for 2 weeks due to serious auto accident—still interested.

Sept. 12 — Mr. Anthony Lack of Capitol Fireproof Steel called at request of Mr. Houlihan, director of Int'l. Executives Ass'n. & SECNY.

Sims wants me to teach 1 hour of a course on Int'l. Marketing in Latin America at Marymount College, Tarrytown NY. My name was suggested because of my familiarity with Lat. Am. cultures and languages.

I sent Sims my résumé, PARs, and writing sample, and will lunch with him very soon.

* P.A.R.s is an acronym for Problem/Action/Results. It is a structured way of describing your accomplishments and was used here to develop a document that expanded on the résumé. In the exercise, you begin by describing the *problem* that existed, the *action* you took to solve it, and the *results* you achieved. Throughout, it helps to be concrete and specific, using numbers when possible in your description of results.

Sept. 13 Reprinted 50 copies of enclosed *N.Y. Times* article to supplement my résumé.

Sept. 14 Called Mr. Stassel at U.N. who told me he needed more time to contact people who could offer me a position. He asked me to call back Sept. 18.

Sept. 14 A priest friend recommended I contact Mr. Joseph Fitzmorris, personnel director at IBM upstate, whom he knows very well. McCabe's brother, Philip, was a classmate in the seminary.

WEEK OF SEPT. 17, 1979

Sept. 17 Called Mr. Ronald Blunt at Xerox, following up on my letter. He indicated that he has been receiving about 10 letters a week from prospective employees recommended by friends and had dictated a reply (not received by week's end) which would be disappointing.

Called Mr. John O'Malley, V.P. at Union Carbide. His secretary said he was interested in my letter and had sent a copy of it to Mr. Robert Walsh, Corporate Director for Management Development and Compensation, suggesting that I meet with him (Walsh) during the week of Sept. 24. I sent Walsh a copy of my résumé, PARS, and writing sample to prepare for our meeting.

Found the Business Library in Brooklyn, and researched the end-of-year report and recent news about each of the corps. from which I am presently requesting interviews.

Sept. 18 Wrote a thank-you note to Mr. Houlihan at the Sales Execs. Club for his recommending me so strongly to Mr. Lack of Capitol Steel.

Wrote for a job interview to Mr. Charles Dore, Chairman of the Board of American Home Products, recommended by Center for Creative Public Service and Dr. L'Cr at Nat'l Foreign Trade Council.

Wrote to Mr. Joseph Fitzmorris, Personnel Director for I.B.M., Sterling Forest, N.Y. He is a personal friend of my partner Rev. George Jameson. I sent résumé and PARS and will call him next week.

Called Dennis, MA, and found out from a secretary (from Brooklyn) that interviews are beginning for Exec. Sec'y position. She took down my address and phone again.

Spoke to and sent résumé etc. to Mr. Stewart Rubin of TASA Int'l., Coral Gables, FL, a headhunter for major corps. seeking people to work in foreign countries. He is a friend of a friend of a friend.

Sent résumé & PARS to Mr. Roger Atterbury of Western Electric, Greensboro, N.C. He was recommended by a friend as an expert in marketing who is always willing to give advice.

Sept. 19 Called Mr. Stassel at United Nations—not available.

Sept. 20 Called L. Frank again. He said he was in the process of lining up the proper leads for me and would call me when he had made the "final link in the chain" within a couple of days.

Sept. 21 Returned Mr. Oliver's call at Vick International. He will meet with me at length after the Jewish holidays and has sent my résumé on to Mr. Louis Norton, a resigned priest in charge of their Japan operation.

WEEK OF OCT. 1, 1979

Oct. 1 Called Mr. Hirschwell of U.N. Development Program at Mr. Stassel's request, set up an appointment for Oct. 5.

Oct. 3 Called Mr. Westhaven, V. P. Human Resources at A.T. &T. His secretary suggested I would get a good response from his aide, Mr. Travis Carter. Called Dr. Kott at Salomon Brothers; he'll be back in U.S. next week.

Oct. 4 Visited Mr. Joseph Fitzmorris, Personnel Branch Manager for IBM, Sterling Forest. He carefully analyzed my qualifications and proposed 2 areas in which I could be successful in IBM:

1. SALES: domestic office equipment at first, then international. (This is key to success in IBM, but may mean starting at a low level).

Fitzmorris will definitely set up an interview in this marketing area.

2. DEVELOPMENT & TRAINING—PERSONNEL

This is a distant second, but a real possibility.

Oct. 5 — Called Mr. Johnson at A.T. &T. and set up an interview in Basking Ridge, NY, for Oct. 11.

Visited Mr. Hirschwell at U.N.—more in next report.

WEEK OF OCT. 8, 1979

Met Mr. Hirschwell, ass't director of U.N. Development Program. They have a large budget used to exchange skills and knowledge (not capital funds) with developing countries. Only a minority of their staff are stationed in NY—most are abroad. He suggested:

1. Passing my papers along to U.N.D.P. Personnel Director, Mr. John Marenki (from Iran), who will call me in to his office.

2. Contacting Mr. Simon Waldbaum, Exec. Director, Industry Council for Development, 821 U.N. Plaza, NY 10017 (212) 867-5017. This group is intended to get transnational corps. involved in the foreign govt. development process and emphasizes agri-business & technical cooperation.

Oct. 8 — Received letter from Mr. Rubin, headhunter at TASA Inc.—see enclosed copy and note *ALL the small print.*

Oct. 9 — Wrote Mr. Waldbaum with a complete proposal, sent résumé & PARs.

Wrote Mr. Arnold P. Monk, Exec. V.P. & Pres. U.S. Marketing—Mobil, using an oblique reference to Dr. L'Or of N.F.T.C. of which Murray is V.P. Sent complete proposal with résumé & PARS.

Spoke to Mr. Donald Oliver of Vick Int'l.—agreed to meet next time he's in N.Y.C.

Oct. 10 — Mr. Joseph Fitzmorris (IBM Personnel Manager) called to ask me to send in a sales résumé and IBM application for position of marketing rep.

Oct. 11 — Went to A.T. &T., Basking Ridge, NJ to meet Mr. Travis Carter, Manager of Management Employment—recommended by Clarke Westhaven, V.P. Resources. He suggested I use his name and contact the following persons whom he would call in advance:

1. Mr. A. C. Sherman—General Personnel Supervisor, N.Y. Telephone—rm. 3217, 1095 Av. Americas—NY 10036.

2. Ms. Anne Marie Shea—Group Supervisor in Management Development, A.T. &T.—P.O. Box 2016 New Brunswick, NJ 08903

He also recommended I use a job search firm—but be careful. He showed me the *Job Hunting Guide*—author Erdlen, publishers Herman Pub. Co. for a guide to search firms in N.Y.C.

Oct. 12 — U.N. Development Program's Ms. Dorothy McAllister called to arrange 3 consecutive appointments for Oct. 16—first one with Mr. Frank Bull. She explained this as common U.N. practice.

Called Mr. François Ferdinand—U.N. Personnel Manager, at Mr. Sabastian Tannen's request; set appointment for Oct. 18 and sent résumé & PARS.

Mobil called. Mr. Monk, Exec. V.P., will be out of town next week. His assistant (?) Mr. Larry Senilman called to say he would like to meet me but requested I also see Mr. James Forrestal, Head of Relations International (883-7400). I will see both on Oct. 18 or 19.

WEEK OF OCTOBER 15, 1979

Oct. 15 — Called Mr. Simon Waldbaum—suggested by Mr. Hirschwell of UN Development Program. Set app't for Oct. 18.

Called Mr. Forrestal, Director of Int'l Relations, Mobil. He referred me back to Mr. Larry Senilman, Exec. Ass't to Albert Sims, Exec. V.P.

Town Lawyer for Dennis, MA, sent my papers back informing me that interviews for Exec. Sec'y were over.

Oct. 16 Interviews at U.N.D.P.—

Mr. Frank Bull (English)—Recruitment Officer.

Mr. Richard Van der Wald (German)—Regional Bureau for Africa.

Ms. Royas—Regional Bureau for Latin America.

Oct. 17 Ms. Ingrid Jorgenson—Director, Regional Bureau, Latin America.

Mrs. David O'Connor—Bureau for Latin American Communications.

Mr. Harry Amundsen, Ass't Director, Regional Bureaus for Lat. Am.

In general, they are all interested in making me Project Director in a Lat. America Development project, but are very interested in my idea of transactional-gov't-environment negotiations based here and promised to take it to their policy board—called the Executive Management Committee (E.M.C.)

O'Connor recommended Ian Fagen at Council on Religious & Int'l Affairs publisher of WORLD VIEW—E. 65 St.

All were interested in Simon Waldbaum and worried about Swedish gov't. opposition. My proper job description would be *"liaison officer without portfolio."*

Oct. 18 Visited Mr. Larry Sendlman at *Mobil.* He is Exec. Ass't. to Mr. Arnold P. Monk, Exec. V.P. now in charge of Nat'l. & Int'l Markets & Refining.

He promised to circulate my résumé among:

1. Development—might involve living in Indonesia.
2. Employee relations—involves travel, but based in U.S.A.

Some responses to begin coming in within 2 weeks.

N. B. 1,300 employees will go to VA in June '80, but 4,000 will remain here.

Visited Mr. Simon Waldbaum, Exec. Director of Industry Council for Development.

He has top connections at U.N.D.P. and with all int'l development projects, esp. in agriculture.

He recommended:

1. Mr. Morris Nadelman, Director, Center for Agricultural & Rural Dev't., 1432 Meeker Dr., Fort Collins, CO 80521 (303) 482–9828.
2. Ms. Yvonne Lecherman, Aspen Institute for Humanistic Studies, 1919 14 St. No. 811, Boulder, CO 80302 (303) 443–1230—publish "Public/Private Coordination in Third World Agricul. & Rural Dev."
3. Fund for Multinational Management & E. (FMME), Richard Sullivan, 68 Park Av., NY 628–3200.
4. Mr. A. Q. Majid 754–5966, UNIDO—Turkish Mission—trains reps. of foreign countries in how to get transnationals involved.
5. TECNOSERVE—CT.—transfer management technology to developing countries.
6. *Partnership in Productivity*—sets up programs in developing countries & gets out.

Visited Mr. François Ferdinand, U.N. top recruitment officer, recommended by Mr. Sabastian Tannen. Also called:

1. Tannen
2. High Commission for Refugees—Mr. Walter O'Brien 865–7602
3. UNICEF—Ms. Jennifer Fielding 754–7980—maybe for Ecuador & India.
4. UN SOCIAL AFFAIRS—Mr. Karyl—for Vienna.
5. Gave me application forms for all posts.

WEEK OF OCT. 22, 1979

Slow week—home sick

Wrote to and set up appointments with:

Mr. A. C. Sherman—General Personnel Supervisor—N.Y. Telephone.
Recommended by Travis Carter, A.T. &T.
Referred me to Mr. Robert James, District Staff Manager.

Mr. Ralph Washoe—Exxon Int'l. P.R. director.

Mr. Leonard Bush—Texaco—Int'l. P.R. director.
Both recommended by Dr. Cifer—Conference Board.

Mr. Walter O'Brien—U.N. High Commission for Refugees—NY Director.

Ms. Jennifer Fielding—U.N.I.C.E.F.—placement director.

Mr. François Ferdinand—U.N. Chief Recruiter.
Who will introduce me to Mr. Karyl, director UN Social Affairs (moving to Vienna).
He will accept my U.N. application forms.

Oct. 25 — Personal interview with a friend, Rev. Nicholas Jordanson—just appointed bishop, St. Augustine, FL—may be a useful contact later.

Oct. 27 — Received form letter for U.N.D.P.—no positions available right now but may be contacted later.

WEEK OF OCT. 29, 1979

Oct. 29 — Received reject notice from Western Electric, Greensboro, NC.

Oct. 31 — Received letter from A.T. &T., New Brunswick, NJ, stating that my application is being reviewed for possible employment.

Nov. 1 — Interview with Mr. Robert James—recruitment for mangers at N.Y. Telephone. They are considering my application (recommended by Travis Carter of A.T. &T.) for their new Management Career Development Program (MCDP) intended to develop new Middle Managers by mid-1980s.

I have complete dossier—if you are interested. Start at 1st level supervisory ($17 to 25,000—depending on experience) for a 2 year *trial* period during which salary increases $10,000. Level 2 brings job security and means supervising 4–5 managers. Level 3 (to be reached within 6–8 yrs.) is beginning of middle management and involves budgeting, employee disposition, *etc.* Many starting positions to become available as of Dec. 1, 1979.

Took 1 hour test: math (geometry, algebra, number associations—did poorly) and verbal recognition (did well).

Nov. 5 — Called in by Mr. James for an all day "*assessment*" consisting of role playing with other candidates and personnel officers.

Nov. 2 — Visited Mr. Walter O'Brien, Chief NY Liaison Officer & Regional Representative of High Commissioner for Refugees, United Nations. He was impressed by my papers and sent them to the High Commission in Geneva for employment consideration. This would involve a permanent series of overseas assignments (*N.B.*—U.N. offers great job security and good pay).

Visited Mr. François Ferdinand, Chief U.N. Recruitment Officer—conversation entirely in French. He likes me and suggested UNICEF will be my best bet. He said just get accepted by *any* U.N. agency for any position anywhere, come back to him and he will arrange for a NY assignment.

He introduced me to Mr. Vladimir Karyl, recruiting for U.N. Social & Humanitarian Affairs—just moved to Vienna. They will receive my application and his recommendation.

Also introduced me to Mr. Vicino, U.N. Legal Dept. Recruting.

I sent an official U.N. application form to every U.N. dept. I have visited so far.

Was informed by Mr. Vicino that U.N.E.S.C.O. is a good opportunity; he gave me the State Dept. address for applying.

WEEK OF NOV. 5, 1979

Nov. 7 & 9	Called Ms. Jennifer Fielding, Chief recruitment officer U.N.I.C.E.F. at Mr. Ferdinand's request. She is overwhelmed with work in Cambodia. Eventually, I was referred to an assistant, Ms. Sally Meehan—appointment set for Nov. 19.
Nov. 7	Set appointment with Mr. Leonard Bush, Texaco Int'l P.R. He circulated my papers, but eventually called off the app't. since he could find no appropriate openings right now.
Nov. 9	Visited Mr. Ralph Washoe, Chief of Int'l. planning and U.N. relations for Exxon. He explained company's local responsibility system, suggesting I try companies that control int'l. operations from U.S. offices: e.g. MERKE, JOHNSON & JOHNSON, DOW, PFIZER, CIBA-GEIGY. He took me to see a friend, Mr. Fred Albright, head of Public Relations in terms of working in their Compensation office, which distributes $40M/year. Stillwell was most receptive but said compensation tends to be a good job but leads nowhere He asked if I would be willing to be Exxon's representative in El Salvador or Nicaragua and promised to circulate my papers to his contacts.

WEEK OF NOV. 12, 1979

Nov. 12	Set app't. for Nov. 19 with Ms. Sally Meehan, recruiting officer at U.N.I.C.E.F. and mailed my papers.
Nov. 12 & 13	Answered another 8–10 ads.
Nov. 15 & 16	Mr. Walsh of Union Carbide called—returned call on Mon. Nov. 19.
Nov. 15	Mr. Patrick Gaines called from NY. Foundling Hospital since I responded to their ad for a Community Organizer. App't. set for Nov. 20. I called a friend, former employee there to get info. and a personal plug with Ms. Janet O'Boyle (She is director of adopting and boarding and would probably be my boss there.)
Nov. 16	Mr. Robert James of N.Y. Tel. called twice to make sure I am at the all-day assessment on Nov. 21.
Nov. 19	U.N.I.C.E.F. interview with Ms. S. Meehan goes well. There are no field director openings at the moment, but if application is kept up to date, openings will be likely even a few years hence (when a field job might be more attractive to me).
Nov. 19	Spoke to Walsh at Union Carbide. He received my 3 résumés—sales, management, training—and likes them very much (they were sent on Oct. 15). He will send them to the appropriate depts. and also *highly* recommends: 1. *N. Y. Tel.* One of his subordinates developed their "assessment program"; so he told me what to expect on Nov. 21. 2. *Brooklyn Union Gas Co.* Both companies hire long range, are very P.R. oriented and need good managers with a knowledge of N.Y.C. people and environments.

WEEKS OF NOV. 19 AND NOV. 26, 1979

Nov. 21	All day assessment at N.Y. Tel. Only 1 of each 25 candidates for the Management Career Development Program are invited to this day. Then 1 out of 4 of these are hired. The day includes: role playing; group decision-making; in-basket exercise; 1 hr. personal interview; writing a company plan. We should be notified by Dec. 3 if hired.
Nov. 20	Called in by NY Foundling Hospital for an interview with the Exec. Director, Patrick Gaines and Dir. Adoption-Foster Care, Sr. Catherine Dougherty. Of 300 responses to ad for "community organizer," they interviewed 10. Will notify later.

Nov. 28 — Spoke to a friend, Rev. Patrick O'Rourke, director of Little Flower Children's Services, Wading River. He proposed speaking on my behalf to a meeting of all child welfare agency directors in N.Y.C. on Dec. 5.

Nov. 30 — Wrote to Rev. Larry Kendall and called him for a Dec. 10 meet.

Wrote to Mr. Vincent Palomaro, Senior VP—Human Resources, Bklyn. Union Gas Co., sent résumé & PARs and will call Dec. 5.

WEEK OF DEC. 3, 1979

Dec. 4 — Called Mr. Robert James at N.Y. Telephone. He told me I had performed satisfactorily in the all-day assessment and was scheduled to be hired soon. There is a Dec. hiring freeze, but he expects to have an assignment for me by mid-January, hopefully in the NY Metropolitan area.

Called Mr. Palomaro, Senior VP—Human Resources at Brooklyn Union Gas C. His sec'y. told me he sent my papers to Mr. Thomas Kreinz, Personnel Manager. Subsequent calls to the latter show he is taking many of his vacation days during the pre-X-mas period. His sec'y. said she would ask him to call me on Dec. 12.

Dec. 5 — Received letter from Mr. George Denny, State Dept. UN Recruitment, showing interest but indicating no U.N.E.S.C.O. vacancies at this time.

WEEK OF DEC. 10, 1979

Dec. 10 — Met Fr. Larry Kendall at Bill Pilder's suggestion. We have a lot in common and discussed: 1) serving on his Mental Health Board; 2) possible employment in his soon-to-be-funded programs.

Dec. 11 — Spoke to Mr. Thomas Kreinz at Bkly'n. Union Gas Co.—director of Personnel. He had made copies of my papers and sent them to various depts. and set an interview for Jan. 8.

Interviewed at I.B.M. (Water St.) for position of Sales Rep.—Office Products with Ms. Dagmar Klein, Personnel Mgr. They next sent me to Branch Mgr. Mr. Alfredo Willman and third interview was to be with Mr. J. P. Meally, Jr.—responsible for all metropolitan area hiring in their division.

Dec. 11 — Called Mr. Joe Murphy, Pfizer Personnel who got my papers from his director (ARMANDO) who got them from the Exec. V.P. (MC DONALD). He said no openings now, but they are future-oriented and have me in mind.

Dec. 13 — However, Willman was convinced I am far too overqualified for the position which could not challenge me: he said I was best qualified among 1500 interviewed, but he could not serve his co. well by putting me in this job. He made a commitment to make contacts for me in the co. more in keeping with my experience and asked me for copies of the 3 different refinements of my résumé—which I sent. He said he would have some report for me in about a week, but was making no promises. Vibes were good.

P.S. Merry Christmas

WEEK OF DEC. 17, 1979

Dec. 17 — Received written notice from Pfizer Int'l that no vacancies are presently available.

Dec. 19 — Mr. Robert James, Personnel Mgr. for N.Y. Tel. called to send me out to meet a prospective employer, Mr. Mark Taggart, Division Mgr. for all Queens Resident Services (88–11 165 St., Jamaica). After seeing him, I am to call Mr. Ray Windham who will be authorized by James to make me a salary offer. My title: Manager of Customer Respresentatives (installation, bills, service changes, etc.) No technical knowledge required, will supervise 8/9 customer reps. working entirely on the phone and using computer terminals for info.

Dec. 21 — Bausch Lomb wrote to say they are considering my response to an ad for Latin American managers.

Saw Mr. Taggart at job location. Looks friendly, will require a good deal of studying, self-confidence and common sense, but chance to grow seems to be there especially since my *Spanish* will be very useful in many Queens locations.

WEEK OF DEC. 24, 1979

Dec. 27	Called Mr. A. Willman, Branch Mgr. IBM Water St. He is still enthusiastically making contacts and will have word for me from Central Employment, White Plains, next week.
Dec. 27	Called Mr. Ray Windham, substituting for Mr. James—N.Y. Tel. Personnel. We set an appt. to discuss salary package, subsequently postponed to Jan. 3 to enable him to discuss my position with Mr. Mark Taggart at Queens Resident Services.

P.S. Happy New Year and new decade.

WEEKS OF DEC. 31 AND JAN. 7, 1980

Dec. 31	Initial interview with Mr. John Deale at American Red Cross for position of Director Specialist—salary about $15,000. Good reactions.
Jan. 8	Mr. James at N.Y. Tel. offers me a salary of $25,000 with benefits worth 48¢ for every $1 of salary.
Jan. 8	3 interviews at Brooklyn Union Gas Co.—for position as in-house Consumer Advocate. Good reaction: salary requirements may be too much for them
Jan. 9	Mr. Willman of I.B.M. writes to tell me he has recommended I work for Science Research Associates, their educational testing branch w. headquarters in Chicago.
Jan. 10	I notify James of decision to accept position at N.Y. Tel. as Manager of Customer Representatives.

This is the final report. Many thanks to everyone at Mainstream.

INDEX